Basic Formal Structures in Music

Basic Formal Structures in Music

Paul Fontaine

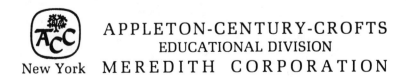

APPLETON-CENTURY-CROFTS
EDUCATIONAL DIVISION
New York MEREDITH CORPORATION

Preface

This text is intended primarily for students of college level who have had at least one year of theory: in most colleges and universities this means two semesters or the equivalent. A modest knowledge of harmony, extending to the more common altered chords such as augmented sixths and diminished sevenths, is assumed. Also, the student should understand the forms and functions of ordinary cadences.

An attempt has been made here to bring some order to the study of subphrase units, especially motives. This and the subsequent study of phrases and phrase-groups are the two most important steps in any approach to musical form. They are fundamental to all styles and types of music.

The story of the elementary forms and how they grew is a sort of capsule history of music. The subject is pursued in this book beyond the traditional classical forms in order to investigate certain unusual adaptations of these old forms. Some of the miscellaneous studies in Chapter 12 are concerned with definite hybrid types.

Great emphasis is placed on student participation. Modest opportunities for original composition (a most valuable instructional technique) are included as optional assignments in the early chapters. The instructor can, at his discretion, add to these or omit them.

The making of graphs compels a student to analyze the formal details of a composition and reduce them to a visible form on paper in a manner permitting easy correction. Here, again, the instructor can determine subject matter for such analyses according to his own preferences and experience.

The final chapter devoted to recent music touches on what appears to the author to be the more important advances or developments in compositional techniques affecting form in our time. Certainly more could have been added, but the main objective was to relate the present to the past, and that, I believe, is at least measurably accomplished.

An expression of thanks is due and hereby extended to Dr. John G. Suess, Assistant Professor of Musicology, and to Mr. Sherwood E. Hall, Associate Professor of Music Theory, both of Ohio University, for reading and suggesting improvements in certain chapters of the manuscript; to Dr. Milton Steinhardt, Professor of the History of Music at the University of Kansas, for helpful and timely advice on several historical and technical matters; and to Mr. Vincent Persichetti of the Juilliard School of Music, for suggesting a chapter on music from the twentieth century.

P. F.

Contents

CONTENTS

Introduction: Melody and Musical Form

The familiar yet mysterious power of musical sounds of varying pitches and durations to thread themselves into meaningful melodic lines is a phenomenon known to man, we can be sure, much longer than history records. No element of music is older except that one which permeates the universe, rhythm. The genesis of music may be set at the time when primitive man began to express himself through a combination of rhythm and abstract sounds. For untold centuries thereafter, judging by the meager knowledge at hand, music continued to develop almost exclusively along melodic lines.

The earliest known musical instruments were nonharmonic, capable only of sounding tones in succession. Instruments such as the lyre and the ancient lute were used mainly to accompany the voice. That man seems to have been satisfied for so long with virtually unadorned melody is not so much an indictment of him, as a testimonial to the central importance of melody in the human art of music.

The history of harmony is much more recent and, consequently, better known. The surviving evidence plainly reveals how tentative and groping was its development, for tones in combination raised problems that at once challenged and baffled the early composers. But always there was melody—in this they were surer of themselves.

Melody may be likened to the trunk of a tree, the branches being the multifarious and lesser elements of music. The primacy of melody has persisted through every style; even polyphony is but the compounding of melody. The reasons for this are partly psychological. One may put together a series of blocked harmonies with the deliberate intent to banish melody—it has been tried—but the ear will struggle to establish a melodic relationship, if only by movement within the harmonies. For music, by its very nature, insists on being something more than a succession of harmonic experiences. In our time composers have proved that any series of tones will generate a melodic action. Thus melody may be regarded as inevitable, regardless of the order or pitch of the tones involved.[1]

Admittedly, the broadest possible definition of *melody* is being used here; this is a necessity if one is to analyze much of the music written in the twentieth century. The word has become too much associated in the popular mind with lines which are narrow in range, move in easy tempi without intervallic surprises, and are singable in a literal sense. But melody, either with or without words, is not solely the concern of song writers. Actually it should include any result of the ever-present and unfettered, though long imperfectly understood, powers of tones to follow one another in meaningful sequence.

Since a melodic line is always present, however simple, complex, tenuous, dispersed, or disguised, all formal signposts will be found along it. When these signposts have been passed, the composition will, in retrospect, present a form. The word *rondo* has validity only because it suggests a thematic order. The same may be said for *minuet with trio* or *sonata-form*. The study of musical form, then, begins and ends with the analysis of the construction and managing of melodies. This does not mean that vertical relationships can be ignored, but the truth of the previous statement still stands: vertical tensions must be relaxed linearly, that is to say, melodically.

It has long been the custom to compare the punctuation of a melodic line with that of a verbal line—notes, figures, phrases, and periods substituting for letters, words, clauses, and sentences. The analogy is apt and useful, if not pushed to the point of rigidity. Invariably the point has been illustrated with transparent, handpicked examples from folk songs. One may understandably become confused

---

[1] Aaron Copland, eminent American composer, writes: "I can not conceive of a music, save by rarest exception, that does not exist primarily by virtue of its melodic content." Aaron Copland, *Our New Music,* (New York, McGraw-Hill, 1941), Preface, p. vi.

when applying the comparison to many passages in the works of the nineteenth-century romanticists, not to mention the ultra-modernists. The truth is that the composer has greater freedom than the prose writer since he is dealing with undefinable sounds rather than definable words.

There is one similarity, however, that is infallible: neither a melody nor a sentence can run on indefinitely without points of partial or total rest. In either case, tension is constantly rising or falling. The line must breathe. In music the points of rest are usually marked by cadences of various intensities. Phrases and periods, which we will discuss in Chapter 2, are the natural results.

Certain clearly recognizable melodic divisions of less than phrase length are so prevalent and essential that they are sometimes called the bricks of musical structure. We will begin our study of musical form with these minute units.

Basic Formal Structures in Music

1

Subphrase Units

The notation of music involves a limitless variety of figurations. In a general sense the term *figuration* can be applied to any linear group of tones which evidences some degree of unity, however slight. Such a group may consist of as few as two notes or as many as the musical situation calls for. There are, of course, great differences in the ways in which figurations are used. In one instance we may be dealing with a mere accompanimental pattern, while in another, involving no greater number of notes, we may experience something of extraordinary impact. Obviously, we need terms at least approaching accuracy in discussions of the various types of figurations.

The words *figure* and *motive* (the latter Anglicized from the German *motiv*) have long been used more or less interchangeably. Writers on musical form have adopted one to the exclusion of the other, or have used both to mean the same thing. There is ample need for both terms, but a distinction should be made between them. In addition, some account should be taken of the differences in the types and uses of motives.

Because of this widespread contradictory use of terms it is appropriate to introduce at this point a series of definitions. Admittedly, complete agreement on all assumptions is probably impossible because of the different approaches to the subject followed by scholars both here and abroad. In the interests of coherent pedagogy, however, a stand should be taken. Therefore the following definitions and distinctions are offered:

Figuration—a catchall term to describe any brief and compact group of tones which displays a recognizable degree of unity, whether it is a motive or a figure.

Motive—a linear group of tones, of indeterminate length, used with such force or persistence as to raise it above the status of a figure.

Figure—any small group of less than motivic significance, whether it occurs in a melodic line or in an accompanimental part.

Independent Motive—a small, comparatively isolated melodic unit which presents within itself a complete musical idea. It is related to the leading motive (*leit-motiv*).

Dependent Motive—a motive which is used with other material to complete a musical idea. The "idea" in this instance would almost certainly be of phrase length.

Derivative Motive—a motive derived from a previous theme.

Spontaneous Motive—a motive *not* derived from an earlier theme, the reverse of a derivative motive.

Motivic Figures—a designation used to describe small figurations, fashioned after an original motive and used in series to form melodic lines (see Example 6). It is less applicable to more complex figurations, which tend to retain the independent quality of the motive and are not subjected to extended repetitive treatment.

Motivic Melody—a melody based on the use of motivic figures.

Nonmotivic Melody—any melody in which no figuration is used with sufficient consistency to justify its acceptance as a motive.

It can be seen that some of these definitions overlap. For instance, a motive can be independent and spontaneous, or dependent and spontaneous, or derivative and either dependent or independent.

One obvious area of possible disagreement will be found in what constitutes "sufficient consistency" to establish a motive. There can be no binding rules as to how many times a figuration should be heard to warrant such a rating. A much more important factor is whether or not it performs an indispensable and peculiar function in determining the melodic content and "spirit" of a composition. A conservative attitude is recommended—a motive, as opposed to a figure, should prove itself beyond a reasonable doubt.

Motives can be identified, evaluated, and classified only by examining them in their proper musical context. Space limitations render it impossible to give, in most of our examples, more than a sample version of the motive. In all cases the student is urged to examine the entire composition if it is available.

INDEPENDENT MOTIVES

Such motives are truly self-contained. They deliver their entire message in a single sounding, although they may be repeated in the course of a composition. The most striking examples are short and may or may not be derived from a theme. In fact, they gain in force if they are melodically removed from other material. Let us examine a few familiar but perfect examples.

The following motive is first heard at the beginning of the symphony. It is inverted in the second measure and is later reflected in various figurations throughout the sixteen-measure introduction. In its initial sounding it is not associated directly with other melodic material but is an independent unit within itself.

Example 1.   Haydn, Symphony No. 104, *London No. 7*, First Movement

The motive in Example 2 is completely self-contained and nonderivative, and asserts its authority instantly by creating an atmosphere of mystery and suspense.

Example 2.   Rimsky-Korsakoff, *Scheherazade*

In Example 3, a three-note motive forms the most characteristic ingredient of a well-known work. It is used more or less continuously in the opening and closing sections, but its independence as a motive is beyond dispute.

Example 3. Rachmaninoff, Prelude, Opus 3, No. 2[1]

The motive in Example 4 is remarkable in a number of respects. It has an accompanimental rather than a thematic function. Like Examples 1 and 3 it is based squarely on the tonic-dominant relationship. There is an energetic drive about it that competes easily with the serene chorale and running counterpoint above it. Notice should be taken of the concurrent motive in the chorale itself.

Example 4. Bach, Organ Chorale, *In Dir ist Freude*

A majestic three-note motive forms a brief introduction to Brahms's Third Symphony. The third note coincides with the first note of the primary theme. The motive is used at once in the bass line, then in inner parts, and occasionally as a pivotal device for modulations.

Example 5. Brahms, Symphony No. 3, First Movement

All of the above motives have attributes in common. All are spontaneous, that is, they are not derived from earlier themes. They have pronounced melodic qualities, firm rhythmic bases, and all are self-contained.

[1] Copyright by Edition Gutheil. Copyright assigned to Boosey and Hawkes Inc., 1947. Reprinted by permission.

A warning should be interjected that such motives are not inherently or inevitably independent. They are so only if and when the composer has used them so. If confusion arises as to whether a motive is independent or dependent, seek the answer to this question. Is it being used alone for its own sake, or is it being used to build a longer line in which it is but a detail? At the beginning of Beethoven's Fifth Symphony the famous four-note motive is heard twice. At this point it is the sole feature, an independent motive. Immediately thereafter, however, it is heard in a rapid series of sequences in which it is only the motivic material for a larger idea. In the latter situation it is dependent for its effect on *not* standing alone. Again and again it will be heard as an independent motive. The changes from independence to dependence and back again are often abrupt but are extremely effective in the hands of a master.

It should be strongly reemphasized that motivic dependence or independence has nothing to do with any physical feature of the motive itself, but is determined only by the manner in which the motive is used. One can add that an independent motive should possess some arresting quality that the ear can readily apprehend and retain.

DEPENDENT MOTIVES

The repeated use of short motives to build long melodic lines exists in profusion in instrumental music. Because such motives are links in a chain, so to speak, the original motive does not stand alone but passes the listener along at once to reiterations or modifications of itself. In such a context the successive "reflections" of the motive descend to the level of a figure and may with excellent logic be called *motivic figures*, since they had their birth in a motive. The status of the original figuration as a genuine motive is secure if it initiates a predominantly figural pattern for a composition or a significant part of the composition.

The following examples illustrate well the common practice of building a melody motivically. The meaning of motivic modifications may be seen at a glance in Example 6. The motive as heard in the first measure is inverted in measures 2, 3, and 4, and undergoes constant intervallic changes culminating in a minor seventh in measure 8.

Example 6.   Beethoven, Ecossaise

A two-note motive is often sufficient.

Example 7.   Beethoven, Sonata in A, Opus 12, No. 2

Brahms's Capriccio (Example 8) may be misunderstood if inexpertly played. The melody, based on a two-note motive, is stemmed up. The sixteenth-note figures supply motion and fill in the harmony, but should not be allowed to steal the melody.

Example 8. Brahms, Capriccio, Opus 116, No. 7

Excerpts from four other highly motivic melodies are given below.

Example 9. Bach, Bourrée

Example 10. Grieg, "Ases Tod," *Peer Gynt Suite*

Example 11.   Casella, "Giga," *Eleven Children's Pieces*[2]

The motivic nature of many such melodies is disguised by the techniques of elaboration or expansion, as in the following excerpt. Here the motive, which is the most important melodic feature of this theme, is simply and forcefully stated in measure 1. It is elaborated in measure 2, and the elaborated version is then repeated twice in measure 3. An exact sequence of the motive occurs in measure 5 (somewhat anticipated in measure 4). The figurations through measures 7 and 8 are obviously derived from the motive. An offbeat version (diminution) is heard in measure 10; except for this diminished version, the phrase beginning in measure 9 is independent of the motive. Measure 13 is a development of the diminished version heard in measure 12.

Example 12.   Chopin, Polonaise, Opus 53

We have examined the use of independent motives in a number of works and several examples of motivically constructed melodies. It should be of interest to include an excerpt from a composition in which every note is accounted for by the extended development of a single motive. The motive employed by Bartók (Example 13) is long enough to be considered a short phrase, but its compactness, and especially the manner in which the composer has used it, soon establish it as a motive. Only the first half of this very short little piece is quoted. The structure is that of a canon with a variable pitch interval. Observe that the motive is progressively shortened and is inverted from measure 13 to the end.

Example 13. Bartók, *Mikrokosmos*, No. 123[3]

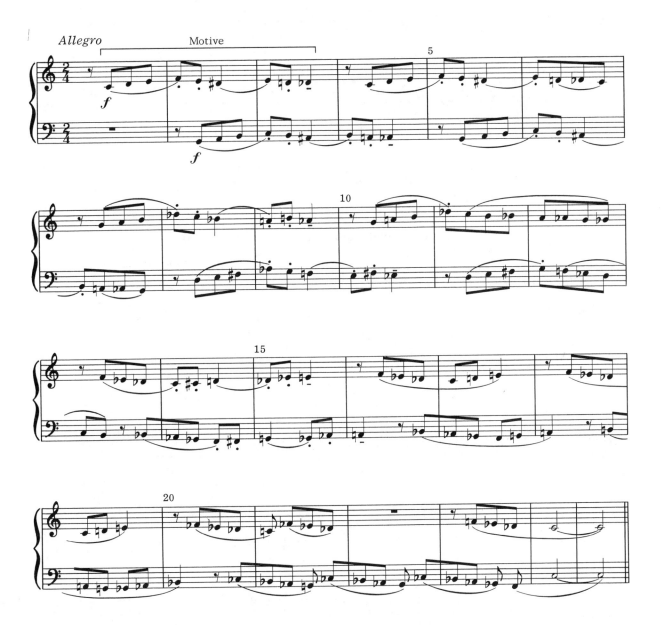

Such motivic concentration as is seen in Examples 6 through 13 is by no means rare, but it is unusual. More frequently, as the following three examples show, the motives or motivic figures are dispersed among other figural patterns which are needed to fill out cadences, complete phrases, or serve as connecting links between phrases.

Example 14.   Beethoven, Rondo, Violin Concerto, Opus 61

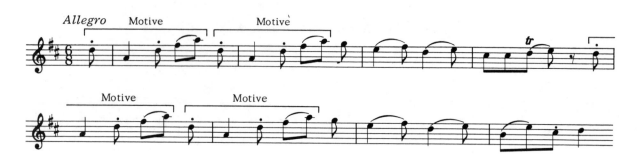

There can be no doubt about the primary motive in this theme from Schumann—it starts every phrase. The figures in measures 6 and 8 can be accepted as secondary motives, an impression which is heightened by hearing the entire piece.

Example 15.   Schumann, Novellette, Opus 21, No. 1

Example 16 should be regarded as a phrase-group of sixteen measures (not seventeen as Debussy has ambiguously arranged it) with an upbeat of two quarters. The measures are numbered accordingly. Used elsewhere in the piece with or without upbeat, the motive, as indicated in measure 1, is the irreducible germ from which the first melody grows. From measures 8 through 15 the melodic line, while complementing the first eight measures, pursues an independent course with no figure emerging as a new motive.

Example 16.   Debussy, Valse, *La plus que lente*[4]

From all examples up to this point it will be seen that motivic melodies may be roughly divided into two categories: those made up entirely, or in greater part, of motivic figures used in chain fashion, and those in which there is a free mixture of motivic and nonmotivic elements.

[4] Permission for reprint granted by Durand et Cie., Paris, copyright owners, and Elkan-Vogel Co., Inc., Philadelphia, agents.

DERIVATIVE MOTIVES

These motives are to be found in the works of all the great symphonists, although their occurrence is by no means confined to symphonies. They are produced by a process of fragmentation whereby a portion of a theme is extracted for extended use. The results may well stand as a reliable criterion of the powers of a composer.

As a compositional technique, the derivative motive came into its own in the latter half of the eighteenth century. The earlier writers of sonatas and symphonies were usually content to repeat themes, changing only the key, in lieu of a genuine development. But once its usefulness had been demonstrated, thematic fragmentation was adopted by Western writers generally. It flourished throughout the Romantic era and is still much used and recognized as one of the most potent unifying devices in music.

As an illustration, the cadenza to the first movement of Schumann's Piano Concerto in A minor provides a brilliant and extraordinary example of a derivative motive at work. The motive is borrowed from the opening theme, where it lies almost hidden between the strong first measure and the climax which follows. Schumann lengthened or shortened it or changed the note values to suit the requirements of each passage as he proceeded.

In studying the analysis, note carefully the following distinctions:

Repetition—the resounding of a passage in the same voice at the same pitch.
Sequence—the resounding of a passage in the same voice at a different pitch.
Imitation—the resounding of a passage in a different voice at any pitch.

For broader interpretations of these common musical terms, see the *Harvard Dictionary of Music*.

Example 17.   Schumann, Concerto in A Minor, Opus 54

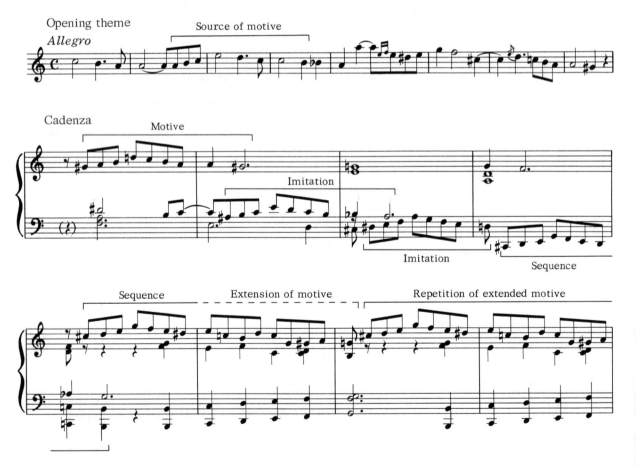

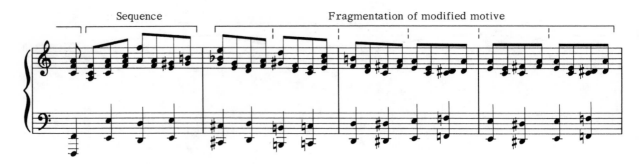

The final codetta to the first movement of Brahms's Second Symphony is likewise a rare exhibition of motivic virtuosity. Unlike Schumann's cadenza, Brahms's codetta is based on two motives. The first is *spontaneous* and is initially heard in the low strings as an independent motive at the very beginning of the symphony. The second is *derived* from the first three tones of the opening theme. The codetta is quoted in its entirety, but is reduced to a version easily played on a piano. The letters *A* and *B* are used to identify the motives in the first five measures of the symphony (also quoted) and the motivic figures based on them in the codetta. Motive *A* is heard both as a three-note and a four-note motive. The use of diminution in the treatment of this motive will be noticed at once. Other features are the overlapping (stretto) of *A* in measures 13, 14, and 15, and the emphatic and independent use of *B* with its original note values in measures 17, 18, 19, and 20 (horns and trumpets).

Example 18.   Brahms, Symphony No. 2, First Movement

NONMOTIVIC MELODIES

Consistency of figuration is to be expected in any piece of music, and normal conformity to a meter tends to bring this about. Such consistency in itself, however, does not guarantee the presence of a motive. The melodies we have just studied are dominated by characteristic figurations which form entirely or partially, a motivic base for a composition or section of a composition. In every case the motive can be easily isolated.

By contrast, there is no lack of melodies that defy such analysis, as in the following example. In building his masses Palestrina avoided symmetrical phrase structure, sequences, and other techniques which might have produced repetitive figurations.

Example 19. Palestrina, Offertorium, *Ave Maria*

But such phrases are by no means peculiar to old music. Any line that moves through dissimilar figurations will produce a nonmotivic effect.

Example 20. Sibelius, Symphony No. 4, Fourth Movement[5]

Example 21. Bloch, Quartet No. 2, Third Movement[6]

[5] Copyright 1912 by Breitkopf and Haertel, Wiesbaden. Used by permission of Associated Music Publishers, Inc., New York.

[6] Copyright 1947 by Boosey and Hawkes Ltd. Reprinted by permission of Boosey and Hawkes Inc.

These melodies are free of the restrictions of set patterns. There is no motivic momentum—they soar without the measured wingbeat. The composer who can successfully sustain them over long periods must have great talent and equally great judgment.

CONCLUSIONS

An independent motive stands alone and is not used to build a longer melodic line. It may be repeated at various spots in a composition as an independent unit.

If a motive is not independent, its use involves repetition, usually modified. The repetition may be continuous (motivic figures) or dispersed among nonmotivic materials; in either case the motive is used to build a longer melodic line. Such motives have been defined as dependent motives.

Figures may be effective locally but lack the generative power of a motive. The term *figure* includes groups outside the melodic line (accompanimental patterns, etc.).

A motive is subject to such common alterations as inversion, diminution, augmentation, backward movement (cancrizans), intervallic changes, or combinations of these, the only requirement being that it should retain a recognizable relation to its original form. Both spontaneous and derivative motives may be used independently or dependently.

Strong motives are most apt to occur in fast-moving music, such as marches and dances. They have a natural tendency to partition a melody into figurations conforming to a given meter. For this reason they are less prevalent in slow legato melodies of a more lyric character.

The presence or absence of a motive is not a valid basis for judging the worth of a melody, which may be intended to stimulate in a physical sense, to amuse, to inspire reverence or patriotism, or simply to exist as an artistic creation with no attempt at emotionalism of any kind. Motives and figurations are incidental to these ends.

SUGGESTED ASSIGNMENTS

1. Find and be prepared to discuss in class examples of independent and dependent motives and motivic melodies selected from the standard literature.
2. Invent a short motive (six to eight notes) and write out versions illustrating augmentation, diminution, inversion, rhythmic and intervallic changes, and combinations of these.
3. Compose an original motivic melody of at least eight measures. Use a very short motive (three to five notes). Interest will be increased if a simple chordal accompaniment in piano style is provided on a lower staff.
4. Listen to a recording of the first movement of Brahms's Third Symphony and estimate the number of times the three-note motive (Example 5) is used in the principal melodic line. Check your estimate with the score.
5. Mozart uses a three-note motive almost constantly in the first movement of his G minor Symphony. Listen to a recording, following with the score, and explain the derivation of the motive.
6. Explain the derivation of the following motives:

Beethoven Sonata, Opus 2, No. 3, First Movement, (Measure 114)

Beethoven Sonata, Opus 2, No. 2, First Movement, (Measure 181)

Beethoven Sonata, Opus 13, First Movement, (Measure 140)

Beethoven Sonata, Opus 28, First Movement, (Measures 199–200)

Brahms Symphony No. 1, Third Movement, (Measures 142–143)

(Note: Bear in mind that in counting measures the first *complete* measure should be counted as number one. First endings are not counted in the above assignments. The derivations must be reckoned from the *first* appearance of the parent theme.)

7. Study the motivic activity in:

Waltz, Opus 18 (first theme), Chopin

Sonata in B-flat Minor, Opus 35, (first movement)

Mazurka, Opus 68, No. 2, Chopin

Second Arabesque, Debussy

Gavotte from the Fifth French Suite, Bach

(In the last item make a point of separating the motive from other figurations.)

2

Phrases and Phrase-Groups

Any specific definition of *phrase* is likely to meet with dissent. A review of texts on musical form written over the last hundred years will disclose an amazing difference in concepts. The much respected *Harvard Dictionary of Music* recognizes this regrettable fact with the observation that the term is used with "so little exactness and uniformity" that a specific definition is scarcely possible.

It is easy to think of a phrase as a rising and falling within the compass of a few measures—a rising and falling in intensity if not in pitch. So it happens in the ordinary flow of melody. But such a concept becomes an oversimplification when applied to much of our concert music. Therefore our definition is intentionally a very liberal one. By comparison, definitions of a *phrase-group* and *period* may be undertaken with more assurance.

Phrase: a melodic unit next higher in importance to the figure or motive. The length varies greatly. A phrase may be contained within a single measure, especially if the measure is of a large denomination such as 6/4 or 12/8, or it may be extended to eight or more measures, depending on the interplay of meter, rhythm, tempo, and design.

Phrase-group: a more or less unified succession of phrases that may or may not end in a full cadence. Many phrase-groups merge into transitions (bridge passages), or are otherwise terminated, without cadencing.

Period: a phrase-group ending in a full cadence. This includes any cadential arrangement, however orthodox or exotic, that brings the unit to a conclusion. We would also include here the single independent phrase which ends in such a cadence and can stand alone as a period as well as a phrase.

SYMMETRICAL PHRASES WITHOUT EXTENSION [1]

Some analysts claim that all music is based on symmetrical phrases. Our music itself is sufficient refutation of this preposterous assertion; yet it is certainly true that a very large porportion of our Western music is constructed of symmetrical phrases.

The grouping of measures in multiples of two is inextricably and historically associated with the dance. In one of the earliest manuscripts of dance music, one surviving from the Middle Ages, we find symmetry of phrase apparently established. The excerpt is from the *Robertsbridge Codex*, dating from about 1350, now in the British Museum.[2]

---

[1] The word *symmetrical* is arbitrarily used to describe a phrase equal in length to an *even* number of measures. The reference is to length only and not to melodic balances or imbalances within a phrase.

[2] A question may arise at the fourth measure since the passage is represented as symmetrical. It would seem that the first phrase is of three and one-half measures and the second of four and one-half. Melodically this is true and should be indicated in actual phrase markings, a rule followed in this book. However, in usual classroom reference, if a phrase extends into a measure and includes the first strong beat, that measure is reckoned in the measure count of that phrase. Thus, in the quote above, the first phrase would be considered to be a four-measure phrase because it

Estampie, (Composer unknown) (4+4)

Symmetrical melody has dominated most of the folk dances and popular songs of Europe and certainly those of America. It was inevitable that this would have a strong formative effect on art music.

From a statistical point of view, the commonest type of phrase fills four measures, the favored meters being 2/4, 3/4, 4/4, 6/8, and *alla breve* (¢). Usually the phrase moves with little or no interruption and is terminated with a cadential effect, partial or complete, such as this one from Mozart's Sonata, K. 332.[3]

But phrases are not always so smoothly and unbrokenly lyrical as the one above. They do not always come off in one piece as a glance at the following will show.

Mozart, Sonata, K. 331

Beethoven, Sonata, Opus 10, No. 3

Brahms, Symphony No. 3

---

includes the strong beat of the fourth measure. The remaining two notes in the measure form an anacrusis (upbeat) to the next phrase. This analysis makes for simplicity and convenience, and it must be admitted that it takes into account the apportionment of the strong pulses, which really determines symmetry or asymmetry. In the case above, that apportionment is 4 + 4.

[3] Phrases may end by other means of punctuation such as rests, holds, abrupt changes of figuration, or natural "breathing points." The word *cadence* (derived from the Latin *cadere*, to fall) can be theoretically translated as any falling off, or terminal lessening of tension, at the end of a phrase. Unfortunately, modern usage has so shackled it with certain fixed harmonic progressions that the original meaning has become obscured.

Chopin, Scherzo, Opus 31

These phrases are made up of disjunct figurations. There may be an honest difference of opinion over whether certain phrases of this kind are actually one or two phrases. The fault probably lies in the inconsistency between the word *phrase* as used in composition and the word *phrasing* as understood in performance. Phrasing has to do with the slurring of tones or the projection of a series of tones in a single breath, so to speak. In this sense it would be impossible to phrase any of the quotes above as an unbroken unit; yet we call them phrases. There have been attempts to get around this dilemma by resorting to such designations as *phrase member* in dealing with such disjoined segments. Since segmented phrases are very common, especially in instrumental music, a distinction should be made between a *simple* phrase, meaning a continuous unbroken melodic formation, and a *composite* phrase, made up of two or more distinct figurations often separated by rests.

Additional space need not be devoted to unextended symmetrical phrases, simple or composite. They are to be found on almost any page of music. A generalization can be made that two- and four-measure phrases are found more often in tempi ranging from *largo* through *allegretto*, while eight-measure or longer phrases occur more frequently in very rapid music. There are of course exceptions both ways. After all, duration in time is a more powerful factor than space on the staff.

EXTENDED PHRASES

The extension of phrases is an indispensable technique of serious composition. Most of its purposes are easy to understand, such as the occasional adjustment of rhythmic balance between periods or phrase-groups, the emphasis of some particular detail of a melody, or the effecting of a more felicitous transition between themes. There can be other and less obvious objectives involved, such as the subtle demands of timing. For reasons that can be felt rather than expressed in words, it may be desirable to repeat a cadence chord, or lengthen certain melody tones, or extend the phrase in some other manner.

The chief mechanical means used to extend phrases, while capable of infinite variation, can be brought under three general headings. They are:

1. *Cadential extension*
   - a. Repetition or prolongation of cadence chord[4] or preceding active chord[5]
   - b. Repetition of entire cadence
   - c. Deceptive cadences
2. *Interpolation*
   - a. Repetition of part of phrase
   - b. Sequence
   - c. Miscellaneous insertions, either within the phrase or at the end
3. *Augmentation* of all or part of a phrase

Extension by any of the above means very often produces an odd number of measures, as we shall see. On the other hand, the phrase may be extended and remain symmetrical, as in the next ten examples. This is especially true of cadential repetitions.

---

[4] *Cadence chord*—final chord or chord of resolution.
[5] *Active chord*—the preceding chord demanding resolution, usually the dominant or subdominant.

Cadential Extension

The following are examples of the repetition of a cadence chord. In the first, a four-measure phrase is extended to six measures.

Example 22.   Schubert, *Moment Musical*, Opus 94, No. 3

The extension of a cadence chord may be disguised or greatly elaborated. In Example 23 the scales supply rapid motion and at the same time sustain the effect of the tonic harmony.

Example 23.   Beethoven, Quartet, Opus 18, No. 1, First Movement

The phrase in Example 24, showing the repetition of an entire cadence, occurs at the end of the last movement. Comparison of that phrase with its counterpart at the end of the first section (exposition) will show that the cadential repetitions have added two measures. Such extensions are extremely common, especially at final cadences.

Example 24.   Mozart, Sonata, K. 282

A deceptive cadence always brings about an extension. Such extension could be a repetition of part or all of the phrase, or a substitution of other material which serves equally well to bring the period or section to a satisfactory close. In this type of passage a prospective cadence proceeds as usual except that the tonic chord of complete resolution is replaced by an inconclusive harmony, which has the effect of postponing the final cadence. An extension then becomes a necessity. The submediant (VI) chord is most frequently found as the delaying agent.

Below, extension is effected by a deceptive cadence. The submediant is approached by its own dominant. Any harmony that will prevent a conclusive cadence may be used.

Example 25.   Beethoven, Sonata, Opus 26, First Movement

Below, the subdominant sets up an extension.

Example 26.   Handel, Concerto Grosso No. 7, Introduction

Interpolation

The next three examples show alterations within phrases which result in extensions. Bear in mind that for the moment only symmetrical extensions are being considered.

The third measure here is repeated twice, extending the phrase to six measures.

Example 27. Prokofieff, Concerto No. 3 for Piano and Orchestra, Second Movement[6]

The *sequence* has long been one of the most used devices in melody building. It is not surprising to find it in so many extended phrases. Example 28 is quoted from Bach's Suite for Harpsichord in E-flat. It well illustrates his fondness for figural sequences. If the student will consult a copy of the complete work, he will find the measure count by phrases for this bourrée to be ‖: 4+4+6 :‖: 4+6+4+4+6 :‖. In every instance, the six-measure phrases are the result of sequences.

Example 28. Bach, Bourrée, Suite in E-Flat

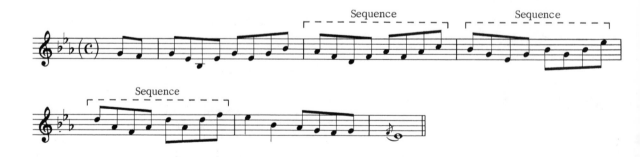

Example 29.   Mendelssohn, *Song Without Words*, Opus 30, No. 4

The phrase in Example 29 has been extended into the tenth measure and is of a type sometimes called the chain phrase because of the run on repetitions of a figure. Notice the overlapping of phrases at measure 10. The *f*-sharp is a resolution of the leading tone, *e*-sharp. It is also the first note of the next phrase. Such overlapping of phrases is often found at interior cadences.[7]

Augmentation

The next two examples show extension by augmentation; that is, some or all of the notes have been lengthened. Obviously, Prokofieff has used augmention at the cadence, avoiding the ordinary way of writing this very familiar melodic turn, which is shown on the lower staff.

Example 30.   Prokofieff, *Music for Children*, Opus 65, No. 11[8]

[7] This overlapping or slight telescoping of phrases, particularly at cadences, has often been described as *elision*. This is another word borrowed from the vocabulary of speech, where it invariably means the joining of words and the consequent omission or elision of certain letters (for example, "won't" = "will not"). This consistency of meaning is not quite equalled in music. Nothing has been omitted or dropped from either phrase in Example 29, or in any similar passage; otherwise it cannot be said that they overlap. Only time has been elided, the theory being that the second phrase normally should begin a measure later. Such elisions, however, affect only a single melodic line. Overlapping of phrases, involving no elisions, goes on almost constantly in a contrapuntal texture.

A more genuine elision occurs when notes are actually dropped from a phrase, whether a cadence is concerned or not. Compare the phrase below with its other form as seen in Example 43, and observe that three notes have been elided.

Brahms, Symphony No. 3, Fourth Movement (Coda)

[8] Copyright 1936 by Edition Russe de Musique. Copyright assigned to Boosey and Hawkes Inc. Reprinted by permission.

The following phrase, displaying a two-note motive, is heard at the beginning of Brahms's Fourth Symphony.

Example 31. Brahms, Symphony No. 4, First Movement

Later, at the recapitulation, it reappears in a hugely augmented version, actually forming *two* six-measure phrases. Some of the notes are doubled (simple augmentation), others are quadrupled (compound augmentation), while the *c* and the *b* are lengthened to over six times their original value.

Any use of augmentation has the effect of slowing a melody. This in turn has a peculiar way of fastening attention upon it. After a theme has been heard in its regular meter several times, an augmented version can exert great power. Excellent examples of this technique may be heard in Bach's Fugue in E-flat minor (Vol. I of *The Well-Tempered Clavier*), Franck's *Prelude, Chorale and Fugue* (Finale), Britten's *Variations on a Theme by Purcell for Orchestra* (Finale),[9] and Grieg's Sonata for Piano and Violin, to mention but four.

All of the foregoing methods of extension will be reviewed at once in our studies of asymmetrical phrases.

ASYMMETRICAL PHRASES

So much has been spoken and written about "irregular" phrases (meaning phrases of three, five, seven, or some other odd number of measures) that the student of limited experience might well think that there is something distorted about them. The first and only necessary argument against such a misconception is that any musical idea that can best be expressed in an odd number of measures is distorted if expressed otherwise.

We have mentioned the symmetry of the early dance music. But when we turn to the great vocal music written during the same years a contrary condition presents itself. Here one looks in vain for evidence that melodic symmetry was an important consideration. If a phrase happened to be symmetrical, it was because of the exigencies of the moment and not because the composer went out of his way to bring it about.

Study the following quotation which is typical of the style of Palestrina (1525–1594). The numerals indicate the exact measure length of phrases to the nearest beat. Not only are most of them of odd length but there is an almost total lack of uniformity. Palestrina did not use barlines. However, the music transcribed below to modern notation faithfully preserves the proportions of the original.

---

[9] Britten's *Variations* are better known as *Young Persons' Guide to the Orchestra*.

Example 32. Palestrina, Kyrie, Mass *De Feria*

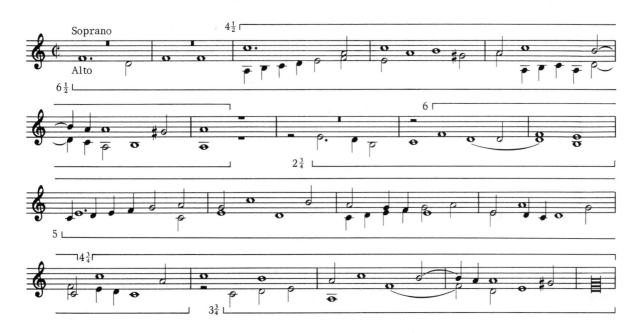

Pursuing this subject into the intricacies of counterpoint would take us far afield, but we should remember that this music is not based on mensural symmetry.

Exceptions to the even-measured phrase to be found in the music of the late eighteenth and early nineteenth century classicists are so numerous that labeling them as irregularities can easily be misleading. Haydn was notorious for his frequent and delightful departures from the usual conformity. Mozart, Beethoven, Schubert, and the other outstanding composers of this prolific era followed his example very often.

There is good reason for this. The continuous and unrelieved use of even-measured phrases tends to be monotonous. Variation in the partitioning of a melodic line, or, more accurately, in the organization of strong and weak pulses, is necessary to the growth of music as an art. It is characteristic of modern composers that they have manifested a growing preference for complete freedom in dealing with meter and the construction of melodic units.

Phrases of odd length may be divided into two classifications: (1) those which show evidence of having been altered in some way from a symmetrical base, and (2) those which are naturally, indeed, one might say inevitably, of odd length. We will treat the two classifications in that order.

Asymmetrical Phrases Altered from a Symmetrical Base

The next three examples illustrate asymmetry produced by repetition of a cadence chord.

Example 33. Chopin, Prelude, Opus 28, No. 20

Example 34.   Haydn, Sonata No. 43, First Movement (Coda)

The extension of the cadence chord, especially in codas, can be, and often is, extreme. The student in search of proof will find plenty of it. He might investigate Beethoven's Sonata, Opus 53, where the final tonic is carried to fifteen measures, or the same composer's Fifth Symphony (twenty-nine measures). It must be said that the greater the length of such extensions, the less does symmetry or the lack of it matter as a palpable element of form.

The nine-measure extension of the tonic chord below is a comparatively modest one.

Example 35.   Chopin-Liszt, Chant Polonaise, *Maiden's Wish*

The active chord in a cadence, usually the dominant, may be similarly extended. Repetition of part of a phrase (in this instance, a single figure) is also involved in Example 36. That portion of the phrase under the dotted line may be considered as an extension. If the example is played without the extension but with the cued-in dominant chord in the sixth measure, its four-measure basis will be clear.

Example 36. Brahms, Symphony No. 1, Third Movement

Now and then the holding or repetition of the dominant chord has been used with dramatic effect, as in the following quotation from De Falla's *Ritual Fire Dance*. The entire coda (twenty-nine measures) can be summed up in one short phrase of four measures:

Observe what has been done with it. Measures 9–12 contain two contractions, or abbreviations, of the preceding phrase and, for rhythmic reasons, may be analyzed together as a composite phrase which is then extended by seventeen measures. The dominant chord alone takes up fifteen measures.

Example 37. De Falla, *Ritual Fire Dance*[10]

[10] Reprinted by permission of J. & W. Chester Ltd., London, copyright owners.

Example 38 illustrates the repetition of an entire cadence. The extension to nine measures cannot be explained solely by the two repetitions of the cadence. The plagal touch (IV) demands an additional measure.

Example 38.   Chopin, Mazurka, Opus 7, No. 3

Example 39.   Bach, Cantata No. 82, *Ich habe genug*

Repetition of part of a phrase is another way to produce asymmetry through interpolation. If one examines the third Aria of Bach's Canata No. 82, it will be seen that the *first* measure of the phrase quoted below is as written. This is not a mere anacrusis. The extension is from seven measures to nine, and not from six to eight. The quotation begins at the ninth measure.

The basic phrase in our next example consists of repetitions of a well-defined motive. It must be remembered that such repetitions do not invariably prove the presence of an extension. Some phrases are inherently repetitious, as in this instance. But if the repetitions push the phrase beyond four measures, an extension may usually be assumed. Stravinsky's phrase (Example 40) cadences in the fifth measure after an extension of one measure. An interpolation of unrelated harmonies follows before the final sounding of the cadence chord.

Example 40.   Stravinsky, *The Firebird*, (Arranged by Frederick Block)[11]

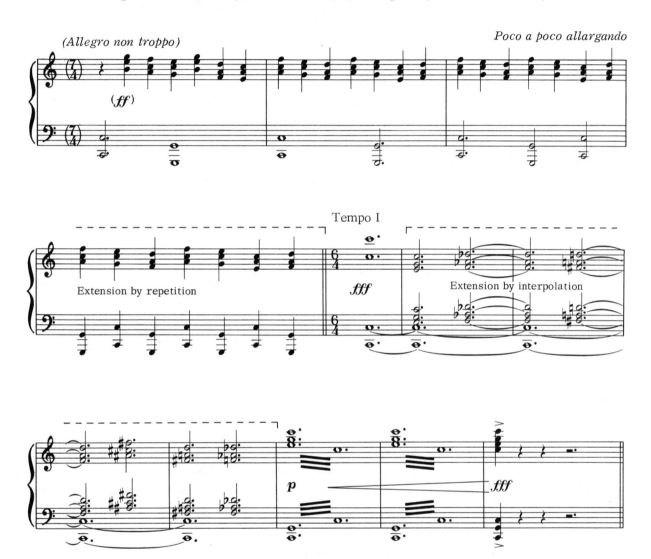

Example 41 is taken from the third movement of Brahms's First Symphony, beginning at the nineteenth measure. Two four-measure phrases have each been extended to seven measures. The interpolation takes place contrapuntally, the last tone of each phrase being held. In such extensions the phrase has not really been altered but the entrance of the next phrase has been delayed.

[11] Reprinted by permission of Edward B. Marks Music Corporation, New York, copyright owners.

Example 41. Brahms, Symphony No. 1, Third Movement

Asymmetry can also be brought about by augmentation. The long natural *a* explains the extension below.

Example 42. Chopin, Nocturne in D-Flat

Example 43. Brahms, Symphony No. 3, Fourth Movement

The augmentation in Examples 42 and 43 is local. Only certain notes are affected. Later in the symphony we hear:

The augmentation now is general, but only half the original phrase is heard. We have augmentation and contraction.

INHERENTLY ASYMMETRICAL PHRASES

There are many phrases which are of odd length, not because of some process of alteration, but because their natural course in a given meter makes them so. Attention is called to the following examples.

Example 44. $(3+3)$ **Schubert, Fantasy in C**

Example 45 is taken from a piece made up entirely of three-measure phrases.

Example 45. $(3+3)$ **Brahms, *Hungarian Dance* No. 3**

Example. 46. (5)   Beethoven, Sonata, Opus 27, No. 2

Example 47. (3+5)   Brahms, Rhapsody, Opus 119, No. 4

Example 48.   Barber, Piano Sonata, Fourth Movement[12]

[12] Copyright 1962 by G. Schirmer Inc., New York. Used by permission.

The examples of inherently asymmetrical phrases just presented should suggest that they are by no means uncommon. Such phrases cannot be forced into a symmetrical pattern without serious damage. One might test this by experimenting with the second phrase of Example 47. Try omitting the first or third measure of this phrase. The melody connects well in either case, but the phrase loses something essential to it. A clever craftsman can "revise" any such phrase into an even number of measures, but this usually proves nothing except that the composer was right in the first place.

Before leaving the general subject of individual phrases, some words of caution should be added about the fallibility of measure count as a basis for classifying phrases. Such classification is practical only when the length of measures does not vary and when there is consistent agreement between meter and rhythm. When such agreement is lacking, rhythm will decide the matter. The following selection, on paper, is a symmetrical four-measure phrase, but this is a metrical illusion. Rhythmically it is asymmetrical. The composer has apparently done everything in his power, through melodic contour and weight of accompaniment, to assure *five* strong accents. The listener's first impression is that of duple rhythm although he will soon realize that this has been imposed within an overall triple meter.[13]

Brahms, Waltz, Opus 39, No. 6

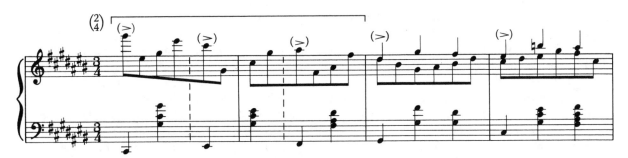

The reliability of measure count as a basis for classifying phrases can otherwise come under suspicion. A short excerpt from one of Schumann's *Fantasy Pieces* will illustrate the point.

Schumann, Grillen, Opus 12, No. 4

One has but to play this passage to sense that it actually is in duple rhythm despite the indicated meter. If normally barred it would appear as below. The phrase shows its true length as six measures. One could find many other examples of ambiguous barring.

[13] This rhythmic division is known as hemiole or hemiola. In simple terms this means the rhythmic division of a six-beat unit into two and three parts successively. In the quotation from Brahms the division is:

In much of recent composition measures are virtually useless as units of length. The meter may be changed with each measure. Such phrases can be judged only by direct comparison with the context without regard for the number of measures.

PERIODS

A period is defined (page 17) as a phrase-group which ends in a full cadence. This is but a condensation of a standard definition which runs as follows: "a division of a composition, usually a passage of eight or sixteen measures, complete or satisfactory in itself, commonly consisting of two or more contrasted or complementary phrases, ending in a conclusive cadence." [14] Such a definition is intended to be all-embracing, hence such terms as "usually," "commonly," "two or more." As a comprehensive description of a period of music, it is more serviceable than the stark ultimatum found in some texts, to the effect that a period is the union of two phrases.

The two-phrase period, just as the four-measure phrase, should not be represented as anything more than a norm. Such norms hold up reasonably well in much of the music of the past, especially that of the classical era, in spite of the thousands of exceptions. However, as we follow composition through the twentieth century, it becomes increasingly apparent that what was once "normal" may no longer be so. Definitions dealing with melodic units should be elastic enough to apply to all situations.

An analogy between music and verbal constructions may be useful, if one remembers that a musical *phrase* is akin to a *clause* in the latter. No one would argue that a sentence must have *two* clauses, since it is known that if a clause expresses a complete thought it can stand alone as a sentence within itself. On the other hand, a sentence may contain *several* clauses. Similarly, a sentence of music (i.e., a period) may consist of *one or many phrases*. The distinguishing condition, regardless of the number of phrases, is that the unit should end in some form of concluding cadence, confirming that sense of something completed which is universally associated with the word *period*. If a single phrase is complete within itself, fully cadenced, and is not an integral part of a larger unit, then it is a single-phrase period. For convenience we will refer to it as a *phrase-period*. [15]

We will begin our review of period constructions with these short units.

Phrase-Periods

Phrase-periods are particularly useful in the following functions:
1. As an introduction, or prelude, to a composition:

Example 49.   Schumann, *Phantasiestücke*, Opus 12, No. 6

[14] *The American College Dictionary,* (New York, Random House, 1962), p. 901.

[15] Leon Dallin defines it well: "Any presentation of a simple, complete musical idea, regardless of the number of phrases it contains, is considered a period functionally." Leon Dallin, *Techniques of Twentieth Century Composition,* (Dubuque, Iowa, Wm. C. Brown), p. 11.

Example 50. Mendelssohn, *Song Without Words*, Opus 19, No. 4

2. As an isolated idea used more or less episodically in the course of a composition:

Example 51.   Brahms, Symphony No. 1, Fourth Movement

3. As an entire part of a composition:

Example 52.   Beethoven, Sonata, Opus 10, No. 2

(Beethoven's phrasing)

Phrases similar to those above are not numerous but it is not difficult to find them. Other examples such as Example 50 may be found in Mendelssohn's *Songs Without Words*.

Often the theme of a passacaglia is a phrase-period. (See Chapter 7.)

Two-phrase Periods

Such periods are so common and simple in construction that little comment is needed. The first phrase usually ends in a partial cadence. The examples selected will afford a hint of the limitless variety that may be obtained by the union of but two phrases.

In the following, the first phrase ends in a half-cadence in the relative minor key. Melodically the two phrases are quite similar (a very frequent occurrence), but Schubert has introduced an incidental variety by the sudden change in dynamics and a whimsical use of accents.

Example 53. (4+4)   Schubert, German Dances, (Opus posthumous)

The second phrase in Example 54 is entirely in the dominant. Curiously, both phrases end on the same chord and in the same position, but the contrast between the two is none the less striking.

Example 54. (4+4)   Beethoven, Sonata, Opus 110

We see next an unbalanced period, the second phrase being six measures long. The imperfect cadence going into the ninth measure sends the music along for an additional measure. An interesting adjustment, not specifically concerned with form, occurs at the seventh measure, where the melody drops to the lower octave. Two reasons for this suggest themselves—it brings the two lines into better acoustical balance, and (even more compelling) Haydn's keyboard had no tone higher than *f'''*.

Example 55. (4+6)   Haydn, Sonata No. 3

Two six-measure phrases may form a twelve-measure period.

Example 56. (6+6)   **Rameau, Gigue en Rondeau, Harpsichord Suite No. 1**

Three-phrase Periods

This seemingly asymmetrical arrangement, while not so frequent as the two- or four-phrase combinations, is not uncommon. Examples from composers of greatly divergent styles are presented.

Example 57. (4+4+4)   **Haydn, Sonata No. 3**

Note the dissimilarity of phrases in the next example.

Example 58. (4+4+4) Moszkowski, Guitarre

Example 59. (4+4+4) Ravel, Sonatine, Second Movement[16]

The following example should unhesitatingly be analyzed as *three* phrases—two two-measure phrases answered by one of four measures. To represent the first four measures as a single phrase is contrary to all musical sense.

Example 60. (2+2+4) Franck, Theme From Prelude, Chorale, and Fugue

[16] Permission for reprint granted by Durand et Cie., Paris, copyright owners, and Elkan-Vogel Co., Inc., Philadelphia, agents.

Periods of Four or More Phrases

The literature of music contains many short pieces which structurally are nothing more than single periods of four, six, eight, or more, phrases. In addition to these, such multi-phrase periods are a very common ingredient of compositions in larger form. The examples are from sources which should be readily available in any music library.

Example 61 is a classic symmetrical period of four four-measure phrases. Many two-phrase periods are given repeat marks. A four-phrase balance is secured without notational alterations. The next step, as exemplified here, is a small one: the first and third phrases are identical, while the second and fourth differ at the cadences.

Example 61. (4+4+4+4)   Old Portuguese Tune (Setting by Corelli)

Example 62. (4+4+4+4)   Strauss, *Tales from the Vienna Woods*

Four eight-measure phrases may form a period of thirty-two measures.

Example 63. (8+8+8+8)   Schubert, **Symphony in C, Fourth Movement**

Example 64, Part I of a popular prelude, is a seven-phrase period. The first, third, and fourth phrases are composite and are based on a three-note motive. The second and fifth are simple phrases, the melody carried in the eighth notes. The figurations for the right hand in the final phrase set up the effect of two voices, the stronger, perhaps, being in the lower sixteenths.

Example 64. (4+4+4+4+4+4+4)   Bach, Prelude, *The Well-Tempered Clavier*, V. 2, No. 12

SUGGESTED ASSIGNMENTS

1. On the following pages is a series of melodies and melodic fragments for study and analysis. Several questions should be answered:

    How many phrases are there, and what are their limits?

    Are the phrases symmetrical or asymmetrical?

    If asymmetrical, are they inherently so?

    If not, by what means have they been altered?

2. After completing the analyses of the given examples, make an independent search for other interesting asymmetrical phrase formations.

Brahms, Ballade, Opus 118, No. 3

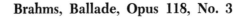

Mozart, Minuet, Symphony in G Minor, K. 550

Brahms, Rhapsody, Opus 119, No. 4

Debussy, *Arabesque*[17]

Chopin, Prelude, Opus 28, No. 2

Use the first phrase as a model for judging alterations in the succeeding phrases. Note the phrase *contractions*.

Ravel, Forlane, Suite *Tombeau de Couperin*[18]

[17] Permission for reprint granted by Durand et Cie, Paris, copyright owners, and Elkan-Vogel Co., Inc., Philadelphia, agents.

[18] Permission for reprint granted by Durand et Cie., Paris, copyright owners, and Elkan-Vogel Co., Inc., Philadelphia, agents.

3. Study the following compositions as models of phrasal symmetry:
   Andante cantabile from Sonata, Opus 13 (Pathetique), Beethoven
   Scherzo from Sonata, Opus 2, No. 2, Beethoven
   Marcia funebre from Sonata, Opus 26, Beethoven
   Prelude in A-flat, Chopin
   (In the Prelude make your own decision as to the length of phrases.)
4. Find and copy down (melody only) a dozen or more asymmetrical phrases from the standard literature. Analyze each according to methods illustrated in this chapter.
5. Compose a period of two four-measure phrases. Take care that only the second phrase completely cadences. Using this period as a model, write sufficient altered versions to illustrate all of the major types of phrase extension.

3

The Three Elementary Forms

The business of composition cannot proceed far without recourse to two of music's most essential elements—contrast and repetition. It is equally true that only a minimal use of these elements is needed to achieve complete compositions. Starting with *one-part* (unipartite) form, an irreducible base, the addition of another and contrasting part results in *two-part* (also called binary or bipartite) form. If, following this, there is a restatement of the first part, the form is *three-part* (ternary or tripartite).

These are the elementary forms in music. The third, *A–B–A*, has played by far the most crucial role in the development of the art because it combines contrast and repetition.[1] In using the word *elementary* in dealing with the above forms we have in mind not only their simplicity but also a quite special meaning. Form in anything also embraces the idea of "procedure." An elementary form is the simplest possible manifestion of a certain procedure.

To illustrate, *A–B* represents the second elementary form. If another contrasting part is added (that is, *A–B–C*) a new form is set up, but *not* a new elementary form. The procedure of contrast was introduced by *B*, and additional contrasting parts merely continue it. Similarly, *A–B–A–C–A*, peculiar to simple rondos, represents a continuation of both contrast and repetition, an expansion of the third elementary form. One could go on adding new parts interspersed with reappearances of *A*, but the product would still be a rondo and an expansion of the third elementary form. In short, every composition has its own individual form, but no matter how great the complexity, it cannot escape its ancestral ties with the elementary forms.

The terms two- and three-part are never so completely true as when applied to these elementary forms, for there are in fact only two or three parts, as the case may be. A longer work may have more actual *parts* than two or three, but if these parts fall into two or three major *divisions,* the composition, by custom, is still called binary or ternary. However, while in an overall sense this is true, such compositions certainly are not elementary.[2]

---

[1] Such designs as *A–A–B, A–B–B,* or the more common ‖: *A* :‖: *B* :‖ combine contrast and repetition, but they are variants of the binary form. The psychological advantage of *A–B–A* is that the repetition occurs in the nature of a return *after* the contrasting part.

[2] If one wished to enrich musical terminology in the pursuit of full truth, such hyphenated designations as micro- and macro-binary or micro- and macro-ternary would have a solid morphological backing. These prefixes have long since been combined with *rhythm* in scholarly writings.

We will now study the elementary forms in their logical order, choosing examples with an eye to brevity, directness, and interest.

ONE-PART (UNIPARTITE) FORM

This first of the elementary forms consists of at least a period. It could be a phrase-period. For this reason it is sometimes called the *period-form*. It is a first milestone in the construction of all forms. Its musical content is fashioned for quick communication and makes small demands on the listener's retentive powers. As a matter of practical composition most of these unipartite constructions are but moments in larger works, such as a theme for variations or a prelude to a fugue or a suite. They possess, for all of that, the attributes of short independent pieces, with a single continuous thematic idea, completely stated and terminated with a conclusive cadence.

In the prelude following, two composite phrases form a period. Notice the four-note motive and its inversion from measure 6 to the end. The phrase division (4+6) is determined solely by the contour of the melody. There is nothing to suggest a cadence until the final two measures. The piece is quite self-contained and independent of subsequent material. Short as it is, it still produces an impression of completeness.

Example 65. (4+6) Purcell, Prelude, Harpsichord Suite No. 1

The next two examples are themes used for variations.

Example 66. (4+4)   Beethoven, *32 Variations in C Minor*

Example 67. (4+4)   Brahms, *Variations*, Opus 21, No. 2

Unipartite form lends itself easily to use in that uninhibited and imaginative area peculiar to preludes and toccatas. Chopin's entirely motivic First Prelude provides an excellent illustration. Because of the speed and quick pickup of the second phrase at the eighth measure (Example 68) there is little if any effect of a cadence at that point and none after until the final cadence is approached. The second phrase is of the "chain" type. (See Example 29.) The third is extended by cadential repetition.

Example 68. (8+16+10) Chopin, Prelude, Opus 28, No. 1

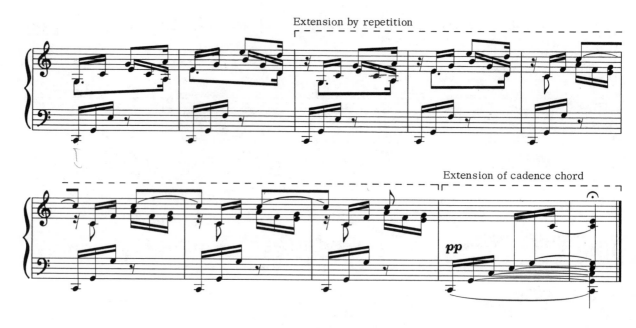

A one-part composition may consist of several small, closely related but slightly varied ideas, woven together like a mosaic without a full cadence except at the end. If no one of these small ideas is sufficiently weighty or independent to stand forth as a part, then all should be analyzed as passages in one indivisible whole. In Example 69 the music moves without a break until the ninth measure where it halts on a dominant seventh chord, which is then heard as an arpeggio resolving over a dominant pedal two measures later. The next eight measures have more the effect of a coda than that of a new part.

Example 69. Bach, Prelude No. 1, *Twelve Little Preludes*

The spirit of the unipartite form can be projected to include certain longer compositions which can, with some effort, be subdivided into more or less perceptible "parts." One such composition is the Second Prelude (C minor) of the first volume of Bach's *The Well-Tempered Clavier*. This prelude of thirty-nine measures can be superficially separated into three parts, including a coda, but the motion is so continuous and the overall structural scheme so cohesive that it can easily be conceived as a single highly fused musical organism.

The study of certain monothematic concert pieces will reveal what is undoubtedly the most exalted use of the unipartite idea in music literature. While all of these compositions may be subdivided into more or less clear-cut parts, they grow from a single indivisible germ of a few measures in length.

All variation sets based on a unipartite theme belong in this category, as do all the important chaconnes and passacaglias. Specific attention may be called to:

Bach's Chaconne for Violin (Fourth Solo Sonata)[3]
Chopin's Prelude in F: five phrases, all duplicates, or nearly so, of the first one
Chopin's *Berceuse:* a sort of ethereal chaconne over an ostinato bass
The final movement (Friska) of Liszt's *Sixth Hungarian Rhapsody:* an eight-measure unipartite tune, repeated over and over, serves as the only thematic material. Monotony is avoided by changes in key and a graduated crescendo enveloping the entire movement.

Finally, the one-part form has long been a boon to the writers of instructional material. Practically every designer of keyboard exercises has used it. There are one hundred and sixty specimens in Czerny's Opus 821 alone. More interesting examples may be found in Bartók's *Mikrokosmos.*

TWO-PART (BINARY OR BIPARTITE) FORM [4]

The most elementary examples of two-part form may be described as the association of two periods. They are, in fact, *double-periods*. The procedures affecting these miniature pieces may be summarized as follows:

1. The cadences may or may not agree as to key. If they do not, the first will usually be in the relative major if the mode is minor, or in the dominant if the mode is major.[5]

2. The two periods, or parts, may or may not be of equal length. If they are not, the second is usually longer.

3. The melodic line will conform throughout to an easily recognized consistency of figuration and spirit despite a judicious use of variety.

4. Modulation is necessarily confined to the nearly related keys.

Our first example is an old German chorale which ideally illustrates the concept of two periods opposing and yet complementing each other.

---

[3] In the Bach-Gesellschaft Edition this violin sonata is listed as the Second Partita.

[4] The two- and three-part forms have long been labelled the "song forms." The author prefers not to use this designation because these forms have been, and are, widely used for instrumental pieces.

[5] Keep these tonal and modal relationships in mind. They were retained in the classic sonata.

Example 70. Bach, *O Traurigkeit* (Bach-Gesellschaft No. 151)

The use of the simple two-part form was very common in Europe throughout the sixteenth and seventeenth centuries and continued well into the eighteenth. Thousands of examples survive, some of the best of which may be found in the works of the early writers for harpsichord.

Example 71. Purcell, Minuet, Harpsichord Suite No. 1

Notice the identical cadences in the next example.

Example 72.   Daniel Purcell (1660–1717), Hornpipe

The simple two-part form was sufficient for the entire second movement (Largo) of Haydn's most popular sonata for piano (Example 73). The hold on the dominant, replacing a full cadence, allows the performer to proceed to the next movement without a complete break. (Analyze the phrase structure.)

Example 73.   Haydn, Sonata No. 37

It has been observed that one-part is a useful pattern for variations. This is even truer of the two-part form, if we may judge by the huge repertoire of sets based upon it. Three examples of binary themes used in variations are given below. They are selected from composers widely separated in time and style.

Example 74. Frescobaldi (1583–1643), Theme, *La Frescobalda*[6]

The theme in Example 75 has undoubtedly set a record for popularity among variation writers. It attracted Schumann, Liszt, Brahms, and Rachmaninoff, in addition to Paganini himself. The first phrase is repeated literally to form the first part which ends in a half-cadence. The only full cadence is at the end of the second part. For this reason the theme as a whole appears to be a single four-phrase period subdivided into two parts of two phrases each.

Example 75. Paganini, Theme, Caprice No. 24 for Violin

[6] Do not conclude that Frescobaldi's melody is an Adagio because of the many "white" notes in the old manner. The tempo should be about ♩ = MM 100.

Example 76. Franck, *Variations Symphoniques*

Eventually the idea of "departure (i.e., contrast) and return" began to invade the two-part form, foreshadowing the ternary form. It is difficult to trace this development with chronological accuracy, and our examples are not selected especially with this in mind, for composers, including Bach, reverted on occasion to these more primitive types long after the fully developed ternary form was in common use. However, the first evidences of "return" were heard at the approaches to the cadences.[8]

---

[7] Play the final phrase above with, and then without, the measures under the dotted line. Is this an extended phrase? If you think so, explain the extension.

[8] This does not mean that all of man's previous musical experience was innocent of ternary expression. Actually, A–B–A constructions are suggested in certain Gregorian chants and even more definitely in later French chansons. Indeed, the most tentative alternating of themes would have brought this about. Our reference is to the conscious introduction into musical forms of the ternary concept, which has had so profound an effect on the music of our time.

Example 77.   Tuerck, Study for Piano

The similarities just discussed affect only the final measures of each part. A much stronger impression of return is created if the *first* measures of the first part are reproduced within the second part.

Example 78.   Mozart, Sonata, K. 331, First Movement

Example 79.   Beethoven, Theme, *Twelve Variations on a Russian Tune*

A common characteristic of small binary pieces is the parallel construction of the phrases which make up the first part. This may be seen in Examples 78 and 79.[9] In these and countless other pieces with a similar phrase arrangement the final phrase (that is, the second phrase of the second part) is a more or less literal repetition of the second phrase of the first part. Because of the parallel construction the final phrase conveys an impression of a return to the beginning.

This treatment of binary form has caused dispute among scholars. Do we have a two- or a three-part form? Certainly there is a statement (first part), a departure (first phrase, second part) and a return to the material of the first part (final phrase). In other words, all of the basic elements of the ternary form are appreciably present. That the return may involve only a fraction (usually a half) of the first part, even modified, does not alter the facts of the case.

The question is brought up at this point because such pieces are undeniably divided by the composers into *two* equal, or nearly equal, parts. Thus, in a mensural sense, they are definitely binary. But they do display a rudimentary *recapitulation*. For this reason, they have in recent years acquired the designation "rounded binary form."[10]

Any of the elementary forms may be used as an integral portion of a large movement. The binary episode (Example 80) is heard near the end of Beethoven's *Appassionata Sonata*, Opus 57. Both melodically and harmonically there is an uncommon parallelism between the parts. The second part is two measures longer because of the digression through the key of the supertonic just before the cadence. Because the passage is unsatisfactory without this digression, it should probably not be regarded as an interpolation. The entire episode is unrelated to any previous theme of the sonata, but its appropriateness cannot be questioned.

Example 80. Beethoven, Sonata, Opus 57 (*Appassionata*)

[9] Are the five-measure phrases in Example 79 real or extended?

[10] The late Dr. Percy Goetschius stoutly maintained that such pieces are "incipient three-part," and should be so called.

In reviewing the numerous volumes on musical form written in the last three quarters of a century one meets a bewildering assortment of types or classifications of small two- and three-part pieces. We have just been directing our attention to two-part compositions. In this general area are such terms as *simple, diminutive, continuous, rounded, balanced, unbalanced, complex, fully developed, sectional, bar-form,* and so on. Some terms appear to be unique to a particular author-analyst, while others have had a long and extensive use. In several cases, of course, meanings are synonymous or overlapping, or are based on exceptional pieces. The following explanations based on observed usages are offered as an aid to the student.

Diminutive: limited to tiny pieces in which each part consists of a single phrase. (See Example 74, or the first eight measures of Beethoven's Piano Sonata, Opus 27, No. 1.) We have used the word "elementary" to describe such pieces but have included also works in which the parts may have more than one phrase; that is to say, a period of two or more phrases and not merely a phrase-period. (See Examples 70, 71, 72, etc.)

Simple: can be applied to diminutive or elementary pieces, but could justifiably define A–B constructions where each part may be a double-period. There is no good reason why it should be withheld from countless pieces, especially in baroque music, showing such designs as $\|: A :\| \frac{B}{a-b} \|$. From a formal standpoint most of this music is simplicity itself.

Balanced: self-defining. Applicable where the two parts are of equal length and show similar cadential constructions. The term is especially appropriate if the approaches to the cadences are similar. (See Example 77.)

Unbalanced: parts of unequal length. Some authors include here dissimilar cadential constructions.

Continuous: music unfolding progressively through the two parts without conspicuous repetition of material. (This excludes repetition of whole parts.) The cadence to the first part is of a type demanding forward movement, such as V–I on the dominant, relative major, or one of the mediants. (See Examples 70, 71, 74, 75, 76, etc.)

It has been argued that many of these pieces are really unipartite with two sections. One could agree without sacrificing principle, but the counterargument is that cadences and harmonic movements are not the only delineators of parts. A distinct switch in the direction and contour of the melody itself may be a sufficient forming force to set off a part. (See Example 75.)

Complex: a union of two parts made up of subparts, the latter being in binary, ternary, or even more extended arrangements, for example $\frac{A}{a-b-a} \frac{B}{a-b-a-c}$ (Coda).

Bar-form: a very old term applied to strophic songs and hence to small binary instrumental pieces of the design A–A $\|$ B. Part I may be given repeat marks: $\|: A :\| B$, or the repetition may be written out with small variations.

A related but opposite pattern is $A \|: B :\|$ so much used in American popular songs. In recent years many such songs have been given a single stanza with greater emphasis on the chorus, which is always repeated.

As remarked above, some of these terms are not in general use and are not mentioned in most texts on the subject. This is understandable for they have a doubtful value. Applications overlap: a piece can be continuous, unbalanced, and simple, or it can be balanced, continuous, and diminutive.

The proliferation of definitive terms may add to the difficulties of analysis without affording a compensating advance in musical knowledge. Some cases, however, seem justified, such as the adoption of the word "elementary." This was done because the word "diminutive" was too restricted and the word "simple" can reasonably be applied to longer formations.

Before closing the subject of two-part form it is advisable to refer to an earlier statement that in cases involving unbalanced parts, the second is usually the longer. One can find many examples of $8+10$ or $8+12$, and so on. This asymmetry becomes at times decidedly one-sided, even to one period being opposed by two. In Example 81 the measure count by phrases is $\|: 4+4 :\|: (4+4)+(4+4) :\|$.

There is no repetition of previous material in Parts II and III; therefore the design is *A–B–C*, or graphing it binarily: $\|: A :\|: \dfrac{B}{a-b} :\|$. This, as explained on page 46 (*q.v.*), is an extension of the elementary two-part procedure and is included here for that reason.

Example 81.   Rameau, Gavotte   (Theme), *Variations in A Minor*

THREE-PART (TERNARY OR TRIPARTITE) FORM

The historical importance of three-part form, with its peculiar features of a departure from, and a return to, a primary theme, can scarcely be exaggerated. This is the basic pattern of modern sonata-form.

Example 82 shows the form at the elementary level. There is a precise balance among the parts. The second part flows without cadential interruption into the third part. This often happens in ternary form and expansions of it, such as the rondo.

Example 82. Handel, Minuet, *Seven Miscellaneous Pieces*

As will be seen, the second part cadences in Example 83. Even more notable, it is a literal transposition of the primary theme to the submediant with the melody placed in the bass. These changes alone supply the contrast.

In most publications of the little piece by Schumann the third part is written out. While the *da capo* is used here to save space, its use is never to be taken as an abridgement of the form.

Example 83.   Schumann, "Wild Rider," *Album for the Young,* **Opus 68, No. 8**

These miniature pieces contain all of the salient features of ternary form:

1. A first part, often marked for repetition.
2. A contrasting second part that may or may not cadence.
3. A return of the first part.

The second and third parts may be joined for purposes of repetition, thus ‖: A :‖: B–A :‖. This duple division of a three-part composition should occasion no confusion—the form is still three-part.[12]

To illustrate the use of variation in the third part, as well as a striking use of contrast in the second part, another selection is made from Schumann's Opus 68. The repetition, as indicated in the example, is mandatory and is normally written out.

Example 84.   Schumann, Folk Song, *Album for the Young*, Opus 68, No. 9

---

[12] Some authorities, with an eye on history rather than an ear to the music, argue that such division is the mark of a binary form. The author agrees with the majority who hold that, regardless of incidental repeat signs, the form is ternary in effect and in fact. There is a statement, contrast, and restatement. Repetitions do not change that. See the first movements of Beethoven's Sonatas Opus 2, No. 1 and Opus 90. The first shows the duple division with repeat signs, while the latter is not so divided and shows no repeat signs whatever; yet the number and relationship of themes is the same in both cases. And who would claim that the first movement of Opus 90 is not ternary? (See page 127 for other information on this subject.)

Variation in the third part may be so radical as to cloud the relationship to the first part. In the next two examples, taken from the suites of Bach, the melodies of the first and third parts have been placed together for ready comparison.

Even to approximate the effect of a return to the theme of Part I, it is important that the first measure or two of the opening phrase be reproduced with little or no change. This condition is clearly met in Example 85. Close study will reveal that the similarities in Example 86 are greater than apparent at first glance.

Example 85. Bach, Minuet, French Suite No. 6

Example 86. Bach, Sarabande *(Double)*, Suite in A Minor

If the divergencies are so pronounced as to efface practically all resemblance to Part I, the analyst has no choice but to declare the form A–B–C. This condition is illustrated by the Gavotte and the Bourrée in the Fifth French Suite. The second part in both these dances is terminated by a full cadence, while Parts III are melodically independent of Parts I.

Because the elementary three-part form lay squarely in the mainstream of musical development, it came to be used with great flexibility, reflecting the tastes and mannerisms of countless composers. The next two examples have been selected to show, in small dimensions, instructive uses of ternary form. In both there is a noticeable trend toward unity of the whole by avoiding strong cadences between the parts. At the same time there has been no sacrifice of contrast.

The cadence going into Part III of Example 87 is of the hocket type; that is, the f-sharp in the soprano is resolved in the bass, while the soprano, after a rest, picks up the next phrase. Notice the overlapping of the phrases at cadences. The overlapping in measures 6–7 is confirmed by the final phrase.

Example 87. Elgar, Theme, *Enigma Variations*[13]

The charming little scene from Sibelius's incidental music to *The Tempest* (Example 88) is presented in an easy reduction for piano. The repeat should be taken once in its entirety, then a

[13] Reprinted by permission of Novello & Company, Ltd, London, copyright owners.

second time to the final measure as indicated. Thus, the form is $A–B–A^2–B^2–A^3$, an expansion of elementary three-part.[14] A^3 is an abbreviation of A, obviously because the descending sequences called for the cadence exactly where the composer put it. A two-measure phrase pattern is established in the opening measures where the third tone of the three-tone motive is augmented. The second phrase, Part II, is of course extended by the long dominant chord.

Example 88. Sibelius, "Miranda," *The Tempest*[15]

[14] The expanded three-part form $A–B–A–B–A$ is quite common among small pieces. It closely resembles the simple rondo form (Chapter 5), the only essential difference being a second appearance of B rather than a new idea, C. Among familiar examples available in almost any collection of popular pieces are: Nocturne in E-flat, Chopin; "March a la turque" from *Ruins of Athens*, Beethoven; *Scarf Dance*, Chaminade; Melody in F, Rubinstein; *Papillons*, Grieg; and *Moment Musical*, Opus 94, No. 2, Schubert.

[15] Copyright by Wilhelm Hansen, Musikforlag, Copenhagen. Used by permission of G. Schirmer, Inc.

It is abundantly clear that the small elementary forms suffer from an inherent weakness—standing alone they are too short for practical purposes. So, as we have seen, they are usually associated with longer works. There, they may be integral parts of such works, or they may be members of a series intended for consecutive performance, such as a suite, or members of a series from which the performer can make a selection, such as the preludes of Chopin.

The material of this chapter has shown that the word "part" as applied to a musical composition is extremely difficult to define. A phrase, phrase-period, multiple-period, phrase-group—any of these can function as a part. A part may end in a full cadence, half-cadence, or may simply be outlined by the musical sense of the situation without specific cadential assistance. It may be thematically independent of contextual material or be but a slight variation of the same material. It is very often impossible to pinpoint the end of one part and the beginning of another: this situation is not confined to recent music, however. It can be found in the music of any period, for it is the logical result of momentum in sound as well as a natural reaction to the "squareness" of interior cadences.

SUGGESTED ASSIGNMENTS

1. Search for examples of one-part preludes or themes not mentioned in the text.
2. Examine and discuss the theme of the second movement of Beethoven's Violin Concerto.
3. Examine Schoenberg's *Kleine Klavierstucke*, Opus 19.
4. Compose a simple one-part piece of at least eight measures for piano or other instrument with piano accompaniment. Use cadential extension. Beware of self-asserting "parts."
5. Investigate the suites of Rameau, Purcell, Couperin, Handel, and Bach, the bagatelles of Beethoven, the short pieces of Corelli, the waltzes of Schubert and Strauss, or any other appropriate sources, for examples of two-part form.
6. Make a list classifying separately those pieces displaying a "recap." (*Important note:* If the recap includes all of the first part, the piece is not two- but three-part.)
7. Locate clearly defined examples of two-part form within larger compositions, comparable to Example 80.
8. Make a study of the part endings of binary dances in Bach's French Suites and/or his English Suites and Partitas. Write out on staff paper endings which are similar, with careful identification of the compositions used, and be prepared to discuss all pertinent points in class. By "endings" is meant not only the cadences but the approaches as well.
9. Compose a short binary piece with a measure count of ‖ 4 + 4 ‖ 4 + 4‖, making the second phrase of the second part a free recap based on the first part. Cadence the first part in the relative major or the dominant, depending on the mode. A modest extension of the final phrase may be permitted.
10. Small compositions in elementary three-part form exist in great profusion. The student should have no difficulty locating them. Concentrate on pieces where no part is longer than a period. Many examples will be found in the same sources mentioned for binary forms. Investigate short movements in sonatinas, Schumann's Opus 68, and the small piano compositions of Grieg, Kabalevsky, and Prokofieff.

4

Combining of Elementary Forms

Once the enormous possibilities of ternary construction were realized, it became the basis for virtually all subsequent advances in musical form. The binary concept went into a sharp decline, except for incidental uses within larger forms as already illustrated. At the same time there was a gradual lengthening of the parts which, no longer restricted to mere periods, became in themselves distinct compositions in binary or—more often—ternary form. They were in fact little movements.

Most of these early pieces were of the *da capo* type; that is, the first part was repeated literally as a third part. The design was used so persistently in the writing of minuets during the eighteenth century that it came to be known as the *minuet-and-trio* form. The terminology is still used despite the fact that thousands of pieces which are far removed from minuets have been cast in this form.

Our purpose now is to demonstrate a form rather than to concentrate on the minuet, although it will be both appropriate and convenient to look at several compositions in this style. It is necessary here to point out that the classical minuet was actually *two* minuets. The first functioned as Part I in the three-part scheme and was repeated as Part III after the playing of the second minuet (Part II). The second minuet became known as the *trio*, presumably because at one time it was the custom to thin the instrumentation here to three pieces.[1] Invariably both minuets were self-contained, and each ended in a full cadence. Part III was seldom written out, it being sufficient to place a *da capo* sign at the end of Part II. As remarked earlier, this practice does not abridge the form. The only shortening was the ignoring of repeat marks during the replaying of the first minuet.

Our first example, Example 89, built around two binary forms, may be graphed as follows:

$$\overset{\displaystyle A}{\overline{\|\!: a(6{+}4{+}4) :\|\!: b(6{+}4{+}4) :\| \; \textit{fine}}} \qquad \overset{\displaystyle B}{\overline{\|\!: a(4{+}4) \dashrightarrow b(4{+}4) :\|}} \qquad \overset{\displaystyle A^2}{\textit{da capo}}$$
$$\quad\;\; \text{C} \qquad \text{G} \qquad\quad \text{C} \qquad \text{C} \qquad\qquad\quad\;\; \text{G} \qquad\qquad \text{G}$$

The numerals indicate the measure-count of the phrases. The arrow ($\longrightarrow$) is an optional sign used here and in succeeding graphs to show that the preceding part does not fully cadence.

As seen in the graph, parts are disposed at upper and lower levels. The primary parts are given capital letters above a horizontal line while the lesser, or subparts, are represented by small letters below the line. Repeat marks and principal keys are also indicated.

Haydn's Minuet is a typical example of the effortless and graceful melody that he wrote with such ease. The organization is very simple: two short binary forms, the first of which is of the "rounded" type (see Example 89). The subparts of Minuet I are of fourteen measures each. The six-measure phrases are extended. In what ways?

---

[1] A comparable thinning out, in dynamics if not in actual instrumentation, is still a routine feature in the "trios" of military marches.

Example 89. Haydn, Minuet, Sonata 15 (Arranged by Paul Fontaine)

Da Capo al Fine

A comparison of Examples 89 and 71 will show that the change to three-part form is more obvious in the musical effect than in the visual appearance of the two on paper. The little Purcell Minuet *must* end on the completion of Part II. The cadence at the end of Part I is in the dominant. A move forward is imperative. There could be no question of returning to Part I with the idea of ending there. It is, perforce, a binary composition.

By contrast, in Example 89 the cardinal characteristic of true ternary form is present—the necessity for a return to Part I. In this instance, the necessity is heightened by the change of key. Part II is in the dominant. Therefore, the only satisfactory ending is to be found in a repetition of Part I.

A more fully developed form is seen in Example 90, where the primary parts themselves are ternary. There is no change of key at the trio but the necessity for a return to Part I is just as great because of the very light quality of Part *B*.

The graph for Example 90 may be given as:

$$A$$
$$\|: a(4+4+4+4) :\|: b(4+4) \rightarrow a^2(4+4+4+2+codetta\ 6) :\|$$
$$B \qquad\qquad A^2$$
$$\|: a(4+4) :\|: b(4+4)a^2\ (4+4) :\| \qquad da\ capo$$

Example 90. Mozart, Minuet, Symphony in E-Flat, K. 543
(Follow with a recording)

Da Capo al Fine

The graphs below are limited to easily available music, which should be studied in the complete score to probe those details of form presented up to this point, especially motives and phrase extensions.

Of the thirty-two piano sonatas of Beethoven, eleven are in four movements. The "extra" movement is variously called *menuetto, tempo di menuetto, allegro,* or *scherzo.* Most of these are definitely in the so-called minuet-and-trio form and occur most frequently in the early sonatas.

It is obvious even in Opus 2, No. 1 that Beethoven was an exceptionally original and bold composer in spite of his adoption of a design perfected by Haydn and Mozart. This originality speaks out very positively in the Scherzo of Opus 2, No. 3 which contains an unusual display of contrapuntal activity and extensions, ending in a coda.[2]

Beethoven, Scherzo, Sonata, Opus 2, No. 3

$$\text{A}$$
$$\|: a(8+8) :\|: b(4+8+codetta\ 11) \rightarrow a^2(8+8+codetta\ 9) :\|$$

$$\text{B} \qquad\qquad\qquad \text{A}^2 \qquad\qquad \text{Coda}$$
$$\|: a(8) :\| b(8)\ a^2(8)\ b^2(8)\ a^3(9) \to da\ capo \quad \overline{(5+8+10)}$$

Beethoven, Menuetto, Sonata, Opus 10, No. 3

$$\text{A}$$
$$\|: a(4+4+4+4) :\|: \underset{or(2+2\quad 2+2)}{b(\ 4\ +\ 4\ )}\ a^2(4+4+5+6)\ codetta(4+7) :\|$$

$$\text{B} \qquad\qquad\qquad\qquad \text{A}^2$$
$$\| a(4+4+4+4) \| a^2(4+4+4+4) \| \quad da\ capo$$

The eight measures in $A(b)$ are divided into two groups of four to correspond to the rhythmic pattern in $A(a)$, but the prevailing figure enters contrapuntally at two-measure intervals, giving an overall effect of two-measure phrases. The sign ⌐¬ indicates a relationship so close that a phrase division is obscure or doubtful. Part B is unipartite with a written out repeat.

---

[2] The words *coda* and *codetta* have long been used somewhat indiscriminately. The diminutive is better used at the end of a part or section of a composition, although a coda may be subdivided into several codettas.

Beethoven, Allegretto, Sonata, Opus 14, No. 1

$$A$$

$$\| \ a(4+4+4+4) \ b(4+4+4+4) \rightarrow a^2(4+4+7+6+codetta\ 8) \ \| \quad (1)$$

B	A^2	$Coda$
$\|: a(4+4+4+4) :\| b(4+6) \rightarrow a^2(4+8) \ \|$	$da\ capo$	$(4+11)$

There is an odd measure

immediately preceding *B*, which belongs neither to the preceding nor to the following phrase. Such measures are in fact *free measures* and do not affect basic form, despite their undeniable musical importance.

In Beethoven's Sonata Opus 28, there are two movements in this form, an Andante and a Scherzo. We choose the first as the more interesting.

Beethoven, Andante, Sonata, Opus 26

A	B
$\|: a(4+4) :\|: b(8) \rightarrow a^2(6) :\|$	$\|: a(4+4) :\|: b(4+4) :\|$

A^2	$Coda$
$a(4+4)\ a^2(4+4)\ b(8) \rightarrow a^3(6)\ b^2(8)\ a^4(6)$	$(6+7+4)$

A *da capo* sign could not be used in the composition graphed above for reasons that are self-evident in the music. While there is never any doubt about the identity of themes in Part A², the repeats are in the nature of variations. Part *B* is rounded binary.

Turning to other composers:

Schubert, *Impromptu*, Opus 142, No. 2

$$A$$

$$\|: a(4+4+4+4) :\|: b(4+4+6) \rightarrow a^2(4+4+4+4) :\|$$

$$B$$

$$\|: a(4+4+4) :\|: b(4+6+4+6) \rightarrow a^2(4+4+4) :\| T.^3(8)$$

$$A^2$$

$$a(4+4+4+4)\ b(4+4+6) \rightarrow a^2(4+4+4+4)\ Coda(4)$$

Schubert omits repeat marks in A² in conformity to an old custom. When the *da capo* direction is used it is often accompanied by the words *senza repetitione* or *senza replica*.

Chopin, Waltz in E Minor, No. 14

$$A$$

Introduction (8) $\overline{a(4+4+4+4) \ \|: b(4+4+4+4)\ a^2(4+4+4+4) :\|}$

$$B$$

$$a(4+4+4+4)\ a^2(4+4+4+4)\ b(4+4)\ a^3(4+4+4+4)\ b^2(4+4)\ a^4(4+4+4+4)$$

$$A^2$$

$$a(4+4+4+4+11)\ Coda\ (8)$$

³ T. = Transition.

Explain the long extension in A^2.

Chopin could have made greater use of repeat marks, but he chose not to do so. The graph follows the published text.

Brahms, Intermezzo, Opus 117, No. 3

$$A$$
$$\overline{a(5+5)\ b(5+5)\ a^2(5+5)\ b^2(5+5)\ codetta\ (5)}$$

$$B$$
$$\|: a(5+5) :\|\|: b(5+5)\ a^2(5+5) :\|\ T.(3+3)$$

$$A^2$$
$$\overline{a(5+6)\ b(5+5)\ Coda\ (6)}$$

The music of this *Intermezzo*, representing the mature pianistic style of Brahms, is complicated by much detail and use of variational techniques, but the basic form is transparently simple. Parts A and A^2 are binary while B is ternary. Phrases are of five measures with few exceptions. (Account for the two extensions to six measures.) The periods are uniformly of two phrases. Graphing this piece in parts (without measure count) and ignoring variations and unessential passages we have:

$$A \qquad B \qquad A^2$$
$$\overline{a\ b} \qquad \overline{a\ b\ a} \qquad \overline{a\ b}$$

Ravel, Minuet, Suite *Tombeau de Couperin*

$$A$$
$$\|: a(4+4) :\|\|: b(4+4+4+4)\ a^2(4+4) :\|$$

$$B$$
$$\overline{a(8)\ a^2(8)\ b(4+4+\underline{2+2}+4)\ a^3(8)}$$

$$A^2$$
$$\overline{a(4+4)\ b(4+4+4+4)\ a^2(8)}$$

$$Coda\ (2+2+2+10+8)$$

The repetition in Part B (that is, $a(8)\ a^2(8)$) is literal except for a slight change in accompaniment. Ravel is at some pains to insist that these are eight-measure phrases. The coda contains twenty-four measures, a number divisible by four, but the phrases most definitely are not of four measures each. The extensions are very interesting. Subpart b of Part A appears in a transposed version in Part A^2.

The making of musical graphs can be a fascinating and profitable adjunct of the study of form. Those given above include, in the author's view, the *minimum* essentials of this method of analysis. Instructors may well add other details such as key indications and the express marking of all phrase alterations with explanations written out below the graph. Studying musical form is a cumulative pursuit, and the benefits of previous studies should be retained and utilized.

It is strongly recommended, if the student has had sufficient harmonic experience, that he write out in full the melodic line of some of these examples; in addition he should include an analysis of motives (if any), phrases (including extensions, etc.), and harmonies. Such an analysis of subpart a of primary part A of the Minuet from Beethoven's Sonata, Opus 2, No. 1, would appear as:

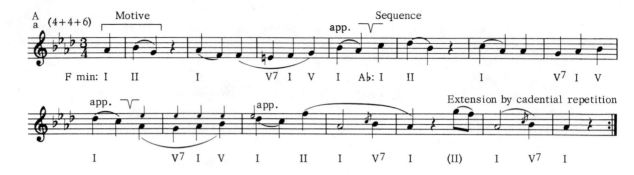

Note: The graphs up to this point have been relatively simple, involving no overlapping of phrases. In later studies, Chapters 8, 9 and 12, it will occasionally be found that a cadence chord at an interior cadence may mark not only the end of a section but the beginning of another. In other words the last phrase of one section will overlap with the first phrase of the next. One would be justified in such cases in counting the common measure twice, adding it to each part by some such graphic means as a (   ) | | b (   ) .

However, for simplicity the following procedure is used in this book. If a new part begins simultaneously with a cadence chord, on an accented first beat, the measure is assigned to the new part. If the new part begins as a partial measure after a cadence chord, the measure is assigned to the preceding part.

SUGGESTED ASSIGNMENTS

1. Make graphs for other movements in ternary form taken from the Beethoven, Mozart, or Schubert sonatas and symphonies, and the Bach suites for harpsichord, cello, or violin.
    More advanced selections might well include:
    Impromptu, Opus 90, No. 2, Schubert
    Scherzo from Piano Sonata, Opus 5, Brahms
    Ballade, Opus 118, No. 3, Brahms
    Rigaudon from *Tombeau de Couperin,* Ravel
    Symphony in F, Third movement, Brahms
2. The student would do well first to construct a parts-graph, such as appears above with the Brahms Intermezzo, then to fill out a detailed graph of phrases and other pertinent information.

5

The Dance Suite

A *suite* may be broadly defined as a series of compositions intended for continuous performance. The word has a common root with the French verb *suivre,* to follow. This definition is about as specific as can be devised and include *all* suites. When we begin to qualify it we begin to limit and particularize. Admittedly then we are dealing in this chapter with but one kind of suite.

The baroque dance suite merits special attention because of the continuing importance of works of this kind by such masters as Purcell, Rameau, Couperin, Corelli, Handel, and most important of all, Bach. As a subject for study it follows logically at this point because most of the dances (or movements) are in elementary two-part form. A few of the minuets, gavottes, and other optional dances are in three parts, with trio and *da capo.*

To understand fully the early dance suites it is necessary to go beyond the external forms and concentrate on the individual characteristics of the principal dance types. We can easily identify those types which together established the final form and, to a large extent, the artistic status of the baroque suite, by reviewing the makeup of a few representative suites by ranking composers of the seventeenth and eighteenth centuries.

Suite in A minor, J. Chambonnières (c. 1602–1672)
Allemande
Courante
Sarabande
La Loureuse (Allemande)

Suite in E minor, J. Lully (1633–1687)
Allemande
Sarabande
Gigue

Suite No. 2 in G minor, H. Purcell (1658–1695)
Prelude
Allemande
Courante
Sarabande
Chaconne
Sicilienne

Suite in G minor, J. Loeillet (1660–1728)
Allemande *4 H*
Courante *3/2 or 4/4*
Sarabande *3 – slow – stress on beat 2*
Minuet *3/4 3/8*
Gigue *any metre*

Suite No. 1, J. Rameau (1683–1764)
Prelude
Allemandes I and II *4/4*
Courante – *3/2*
Gigue *2/1*
Sarabandes I and II *3/2 or 3/4*
Venitienne
Gavotte – *¢ begin mid-measure*
Minuet

Suite (Ordre) No. 8, F. Couperin (1668–1733)
La Raphael (Prelude)
Allemande
Courantes I and II
Sarabande
Gavotte
Rondeau
Gigue
Passacaglia
La Morinette

This should be enough to suggest that four dance types overshadow all others—the allemande, the courante, the sarabande and the gigue. In the suites of Rameau and Couperin the presence of these dances is sometimes hidden under a fanciful title. For instance, the piece *La Morinette* (see above) is in the style of a gigue.

The evidence is overwhelming in the suites of Handel and Bach. Handel left sixteen suites for harpsichord in which we find twelve allemandes, ten courantes, six sarabandes, and twelve gigues, a total far outnumbering all other dances. He occasionally substituted a free adagio or largo for the sarabande. When we add this to the fact that Bach, supreme master of the suite, used all four of these dance types in his suites, with relatively few exceptions, then it can be readily understood why these particular dances are regarded as the "fixed" members of the baroque suite and why they should be placed at the top of our list for study.

Certain general facts should be known and remembered.

1. Most of Bach's suites and partitas exhibit a prelude, although it may be called an overture, sinfonia, preambule, toccata, or fantasia, depending in some measure on the style of the music. None of these is based on a dance.

2. With extremely rare exceptions, all members of a given suite are in the same key. (Sometimes Couperin alternated between the parallel modes.)

3. The fixing of the order of the dances required the experience of many years, and is a matter for a history rather than for this book. For our purposes it may simply be stated that the order favored by Bach presents the material with the greatest possible contrasts in rhythm, mood, and tempo. The four fixed dance types will be introduced in the order they usually hold in the suite.

ALLEMANDE

This is generally assumed to be a German dance, an assumption that may be resting too heavily on the circumstance that the name (in French) means "German." Some authorities doubt that the allemande, as we know it in the baroque suite, is based on a dance at all. Be that as it may, the meter is 4/4 with a short upbeat and the form binary. As is the case with all these dances, one encounters vast differences in personal styles. However, unless there is a prelude, the allemande invariably appears at the beginning of the suite.

Purcell's Allemande is as smooth and regular as a gavotte or bourrée.

Example 91. Purcell, Allemande, Harpsichord Suite No. 1

Handel (Example 92) sets forth in quite a different manner, with a mild use of imitation.

Example 92. Handel, Allemande, Harpsichord Suite No. 8

With Bach the allemande became the least dance-like of all the fixed members of the suite. He treated it in a free contrapuntal rather than a strictly polyphonic style.

Example 93. Bach, Allemande, French Suite No. 2

COURANTE (CORRENTE)

The earliest surviving example of a courante dates from the middle of the sixteenth century. The dance appears to have gone out of fashion about the year 1700.

There are two types of courante appearing in the Bach suites—the French type, previously developed by Chambonnières, Lully, and others, in 6/4 or 3/2 meter; and the Italian corrente in 3/4 or 3/8, examples of which may be found in the *Sonate da Camera* of Corelli.

If we may judge by numbers alone, Bach had a preference for the French type. Perhaps he was intrigued by the subtle cross accents resulting from the interplay of 6/4 and 3/2. The use of 6/4 means a duple division of the bar, approximating two measures of 3/4, while 3/2 means a triple division. This use of the hemiola was common in these dances. Sometimes the duple and triple divisions are opposed, as in the following example.

Example 94. Bach, Courante (Second *Double*), English Suite No. 1

The words *courante* and *corrente* (French and Italian respectively) are derived from a common Latin root meaning "to run." We may infer that these dances were very energetic affairs. This impression is much stronger in the corrente. In fact, that dance differs so greatly from the French dance of the same name that it is difficult to credit the claim that both evolved from the same source. The corrente carries out the *moto perpetuo* idea. It usually consists of *continuous* eighth notes, triplet eighths, or sixteenths.

Example 95.   Corelli, Corrente, *Sonata da Camera* No. 3

Without question the corrente presents the greater contrast to the allemande. The courante, while differing in meter, often resembles the allemande in general style and texture.[1] To be sure, it moves at a somewhat faster pace.

SARABANDE

This dance probably came into Europe through Spain. Its name suggests a Moorish or Saracenic origin. Whatever may have been the nature of the first sarabande, or zarabanda, the dance came into the baroque suite as a slow movement in 3/4 or 3/2 meter.

A peculiar feature of the true sarabande is the frequent stress on the second beat.

Example 96.   Couperin, Suite No. 1 (Premier ordre)

Example 97.   Bach, French Suite No. 4

[1] Compare the courantes and allemandes of the First and Second English Suites, then do the same with the Fifth French Suite. In the last we find a true corrente, though in some editions the title "courante" is inappropriately used. See Spitta's *Johann Sebastian Bach*, New York, Dover, 1951, vol. II, p. 85.

No other member of the baroque suite has had so far-reaching an influence on later music as the sarabande. Let us look at a few themes which are not known as sarabandes but which show an unmistakable resemblance.

Bach, Chaconne for Violin

Haydn, Adagio, Piano Sonata No. 52

Mozart, *Jupiter* Symphony, K. 551, Second Movement

Brahms, Symphony No. 1, Second Movement

Debussy, *Clair de Lune*[2]

GIGUE (GIGA, JIG)

It is certain that long before the end of the sixteenth century every country in Europe had its counterpart of the gigue. To single out a country as its place of origin is risky. However, Italy is commonly accorded the honor.

Wherever it was known, the gigue was a dance of movement rather than refinement. Its later popularity as a finale for the suite was an international recognition that a program—a suite is a program—is most fittingly ended in an *allegro* spirit. In those suites where the gigue is lacking, its place may be competently taken by a rondo, a hornpipe, a passepied, or some other music of a rapid nature.

There is no specific meter for the gigue. In the Bach clavier suites alone we find 3/8, 6/8, 12/8, 9/16, 12/16, 2/1, and 4/4. This in itself suggests a multiplicity of sources. Once the gigue was adopted into serious music, the matter of meter was no longer important, if it ever had been. The one unfailing characteristic of all gigues is fast-moving melody expressed in triplet or dotted-note figures, and this can be accommodated to any meter.

As could have been expected, when the gigue came under the hand of Bach it took on a new dignity. In some instances, such as the Fifth French Suite, the gigue overshadows all the other movements.

One of Bach's favorite contrivances in writing a two-part gigue may be seen in this Fifth French Suite. Dividing the composition into two nearly equal parts, he uses an inversion of the first theme as a subject for the second part.

Incidentally, both parts are in fugal style, that is, successive "voices" take up the theme in imitation of the first voice, a feature to be observed in several of Bach's gigues.

Example 98.   Bach, Gigue, French Suite No. 5

Theme as heard in first part

As inverted in second part

[2] Permission for reprint granted by Editions Jean Jobert, Paris, copyright owners, and Elkan-Vogel Co., Inc., Philadelphia, agents.

The influence of the gigue on music other than the suite is difficult to assess. Even when Bach was writing his suites, composers of sonatas were writing last movement allegros and prestos which were not gigues. On the other hand, one can find final movements in late classical and early romantic sonatas which contain themes strongly reminiscent of the gigue. (See Beethoven's Pianoforte Sonatas Opus 2, No. 1 and Opus 31, No. 3; also Schubert's Grand Sonata in C minor.)

The effective addition of optional dances to the four traditional types just reviewed required time and experimentation. The joining of the moderate allemande and the more rapid courante, or corrente, was a natural development. There were precedents for this, such as the pavan-galliard combination of the English virginalists and the slow-fast sectioning of the French overture.

The clear need for a slower movement after the courante soon established the position of the sarabande. But it is after the sarabande that we find the earliest writers of suites in apparent indecision. Neither Rameau nor Couperin ever revealed a comprehensive grasp of the suite as an entity. Couperin spun together rondos, gigues, or airs (most of them with descriptive titles) quite at random. In fact, his second suite lists twenty-three pieces. In justice to him it must be remarked that he called these marathon assemblages *ordres* (which can be translated as "collections of pieces") rather than suites.

It remained for the German composers, and especially Bach, to fashion the components of the suite into a more or less standard and interrelated sequence. These men seemed to feel instinctively that the arrangement allemande-courante-sarabande-gigue was out of balance. The weakness was between the sarabande and the gigue.

There was a rich assortment of dances at hand from which to choose a remedy. But whatever was chosen would have to move more slowly and with less excitement than the gigue and yet offer an enlivened contrast to the sarabande. Then the tempi balance would be somewhat as follows:

A		B	C	
Moderate	Fast	Slow	Moderate	Fast
allemande	courante	sarabande	?	gigue

A tripartite division within the suite was emerging which presaged the sonata.

The favored optional choices settled on the minuet, the gavotte, the bourrée, and the passepied, all importations from France. These may also be called the "trio" dances because they were so often presented in pairs, that is, a first dance, then a second one of the same type, followed by a repetition (*da capo*) of the first, in the familiar minuet-and-trio procedure.

MINUET

The minuet has already been studied as a form in Chapter 4. It can only be added that as a ballroom dance it was distinguished for its grace, elegance, and unhurried movement. These attributes are reflected in the music of any typical minuet with its felicity of melody. The directive *alla menuetto* on any piece of music is a command for a controlled tempo and attention to the ingratiating spirit of the dance. The meter is always triple, and departures from phrasal symmetry are rare even in concert minuets.

The history of the minuet as an idealized dance is unique. It is the only member of the suite to pass into the sonata intact and under its own name. At first its position in its new environment was uncertain. Haydn wrote fifty-two clavier sonatas, most of them in three movements. The minuet may be found as a final movement or in the second position in lieu of an andante. In his last sonatas he abandoned the minuet, but retained it as a third movement in his quartets and symphonies, as did Mozart.[3] The restrained pace of the minuet did not long satisfy Beethoven. He soon replaced it with the livelier scherzo.

---

[3] Occasionally the minuet serves as the second of four movements. See Mozart's Quintets, K. 515 and 516. Also Mendelssohn's Quartet, Opus 44, No. 1. This change is also reflected in Chopin's piano sonatas where the scherzo precedes the slow movement.

GAVOTTE

The gavotte became very popular throughout Europe during the eighteenth century. In its most prototypal form it is in *alla breve* meter with phrases beginning at mid-measure.

Example 99.   Bach, Gavotte, Cello Suite No. 6

A feature of many gavottes is the musette, which could be described as a trio with a drone bass. The name is French for "bagpipe," which instantly explains its aptness. This style of accompaniment, usually preceded by the directive *à la musette,* has long since been adopted in other forms and meters. It is nothing more than a pedal bass either droned (held) or repeated at more or less regular intervals. In more advanced applications of the idea, the held tone or tones may be in the treble.[4]

BOURRÉE

The bourrée is similar to the gavotte in all practical respects except that the phrases begin with a quarter-measure upbeat.

Example 100.   Bach, Bourrée, Violin Partita No. 1

PASSEPIED

The baroque passepied is in rapid 3/8 meter. It has been described as a fast minuet. There are questionable "minuets" in this meter (see Handel's Suite 14) as well as a large number of "allegros" which could reasonably have been labeled as passepieds.[5]

---

[4] An example of a musette as the trio of a minuet may be seen in Ravel's Suite *Tombeau de Couperin* (piano).

[5] Certain pieces called passepieds in *alla breve* meter have been written by late French composers. See the passepied from the opera, *Le Roi s'amuse* by Delibes and the last movement of Debussy's *Suite bergamasque.*

Example 101. Bach, Passepied, First Suite for Orchestra

In a *double* for this passepied Bach adds a corrente-style running counterpoint.

The early writers of partitas interpreted the form according to the Italian concept, that is, as a series of variations. In time the words "partita" and "suite" became confused and eventually synonymous. Handel retained something of the old partita idea in his clavier suites. This is frequently noticeable in the opening measures of the allemande, and the courante. In his Fourth Suite there is a definite thematic bond linking the Allemande, the Courante and the Gigue.

But these small similarities are evident only in the initial measures and are not pursued with the conscious consistency of real variations. The Bach partitas for harpsichord are quite frankly suites.

Most of Bach's instrumental works were composed at Cöthen (1717–1723). The experimental spirit was always with him. As a result, his suites and partitas are not all of a single pattern. The best balanced are the French Suites and those for solo cello. Both sets follow a consistent order, the only variation being in the selection of optional dances.

The preludes of the English Suites are progressively longer until, in the Sixth Suite, the Prelude alone accounts for over half the total length. This disproportion is not so noticeable in the playing time as it is on paper.

The four orchestral suites are also called overtures. Here Bach turns away from the old fixed dance types, limiting himself to a Courante in the First Suite, a Sarabande in the Second, and a Gigue in the Third. All the other movements are optional types or pieces not related to any dance. The Arioso of the Third Suite for Orchestra is one of Bach's most celebrated inspirations.

SUGGESTED ASSIGNMENTS

1. Be prepared to discuss in class the outstanding characteristics of the dances most used in the baroque suite.
2. In addition, familiarize yourself with the following optional types:
    Air (Aria or Arioso)
    Bolero
    Forlane (Forlana) (See Bach's Orchestral Suite No. 1)
    Galliard (See *Fitzwilliam Virginal Book*)
    Hornpipe
    Intrada
    Loure (See Bach's French Suite No. 5)
    Pavane
    Polonaise
    Rigaudon (or Rigadoon)
    Sicilienne
3. Listen to the Second Passepied of Bach's Orchestral Suite No. 1 and compare it to a corrente.
4. Search through the movements of sonatas, symphonies, or miscellaneous compositions, for examples of plausible influences of, or similarities to, the old baroque dance types. In all cases bring these to the instructor.
5. An excellent exercise for class use is the playing, preferably on the piano, of excerpts from many old suites of various countries for the students to identify by type. They must depend solely on the ear, and the answers will not always be "correct" according to the composer, since there is a close resemblance between some of the dances while others are practically identical. A rigaudon could honestly be called a bourrée. A tarantella, a rapid dance in 6/8 meter not native to the baroque suite, could be mistaken for a jig. Vary the material with extracts from sonatas, symphonies, or the literature in general which bear a plausible kinship to any standard type found in the baroque suite. In these cases, the instructor will have to serve as judge.

6

The Simple Rondo[1]

If the third elementary form (*A–B–A*) is extended by a *second* contrasting part and a *third* sounding of the first part, the resulting design (*A–B–A–C–A*) is that of the shortest possible rondo. The contrasting parts (*B, C,* etc.) may be defined as *intermezzi* or *episodes*. (In the old French *rondeaux* they were called *couplets.*) Part A not only sets the spirit of the piece at the beginning but serves as a ritornello, or "returning" theme, after each episode, a function implicit in the word "rondo."

The procedure of alternating the first or principal theme with episodes may be extended indefinitely, but it cannot be reduced below the formula given above and fall within the definition of a rondo. In some of the early rondos the principal theme, always brief, may be heard half a dozen times or more. For example, in Couperin's Passacaglia en rondeau it is heard nine times.

It is not surprising that so many of these old rondos are but successions of small unipartite ideas, each ending in a cadence, partial or complete. The attractive possibilities of the art of transition, so closely associated with later rondos, were not yet fully realized.

Our first example, selected from Rameau, is superior to most rondos of his time both in musical quality and construction. The first episode (*B*) ends in a half-cadence, the second (*C*) in a full cadence, while the third (*D*) shows a real transition to the final statement (via *da capo*) of the principal theme. The design is *A–B–A–C–A–D–A*. Note that this rondo is also a musette and that it is in 3/4 meter. The tonic tone is sounded in the bass in almost every measure. Thus it may be seen again that the musette style of accompaniment is not restricted as to meter or type of composition.

Since Rameau makes no notational changes whatever in any of the repetitions of Part A, it is possible to present this rondo in a minimum of space with three *da capo* signs. The player should remember that nothing is to be repeated except Part A.

This little rondo is typical of thousands of others written during the seventeenth and eighteenth centuries. There are other good examples in the works of Couperin and the sonatinas of Clementi and Kuhlau, as well as the sonatas of Haydn and Mozart.

Example 102. Rameau, Musette en Rondeau, Harpsichord Suite No. 1

[1] That is, the simple rondo as opposed to the sonata-rondo (Chapter 9).

Because so many rondos move at *allegro* speeds and are musically shallow, it has sometimes been flatly stated that these are the normal characteristics of a rondo, or at least of a "genuine" rondo. This is confusing content with form. The truth is that a large number of rondos move slowly and are anything but gay and trivial. Several excellent examples of this nature are included in the list at the end of this chapter. This point can be emphasized and our knowledge of the form advanced at the same time by turning our attention to the first eight measures of Mozart's Rondo in A minor.

Example 103.   Mozart, Rondo in A Minor

This is an independent composition unassociated with other movements and is included in any representative collection of Mozart's miscellaneous works. Aside from its great merit as music, the student should be interested in the following formal details. Part *A* is ternary. Only the first period is used in A^2. The contrasting episodes (*B* and *C*) are prolonged and highly developed, considerably exceeding the combined length of all appearances of *A*. In *C* nine measures are marked for repetition, and there is a codetta of thirteen measures. The transitions from *B* and *C* to A^2 and A^3 respectively should be carefully studied in the music itself.

Mozart, Rondo in A Minor

$$\underset{a(8)\ b(14)\ a^2(8)}{A} \qquad \underset{a(23)\ a^2(27)}{B} \rightarrow \underset{a(8)}{A^2}$$

$$\underset{\|: a(9) :\|\ b(6)\ a^2(12)\ codetta(13}{C} \rightarrow \underset{a(8)\ b(14)\ a^2(12)}{A^3}$$

$$Coda\ (20)$$

Mozart's rondo is a vast advance from that of Rameau in every respect except clarity of form. Both are simple rondos, with the latter having three episodes instead of two. In neither rondo is there a change of key in any of the ritornelli. Mozart introduced some ornamentation of the melodic line in Part A^3. The opportunity to heighten interest and guard against monotony in the rondo form by the use of variational techniques was seized on occasion not only by Mozart but also by Bach, Beethoven, and Brahms.

With this in mind let us examine briefly the first theme and its subsequent returns in Brahms's Capriccio, Opus 76, No. 2, a piece that happens to be in the form of a simple rondo. In this text only the first four measures of the theme will be used. This will suffice for purposes of comparison, but the student is advised to review the composition in its entirety.

Example 104. Brahms, Capriccio, Opus 76, No. 2

(*A*) The following is the principal theme as it first appears. Notice the chromatic bass line.

(*A²*) There is little change in the upper part, but the bass line is reinforced by broken octaves and moved to a higher register.

(*A³*) The melody has been considerably altered and is assigned to an inner voice. The chromatic line, formerly in the bass, is now in the soprano.

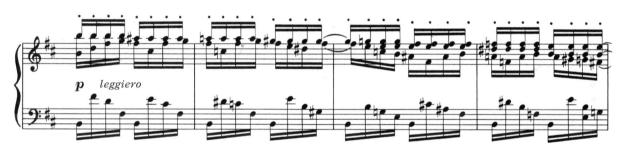

In Part *A³* the theme is repeated just as it is in Part *A*. However, here the repetition is heard as a final variation. The phrase is distributed through a series of changes of register.[2] The chromatic line is still discernible in the lower tones of the chords which fall on the beats.

[2] The word "register" as used here means the pitch range of an octave.

Other examples of the use of variation techniques in ritornellos are cited in a suggested list of pieces in rondo form. Analyze and discuss as many of these pieces as are available. Some are not known as rondos, but form is not dependent on titles. As a group they reveal the versatility and value of the simple rondo design.

Keep in mind that unity is the basic function of the ritornello to be opposed by the normal variety that comes with the episodes. If the episodes are too brief or there are too many recurrences of the ritornello, monotony may result (and does result in many of the old rondos). Composers enhance the element of variety by optional techniques such as shortening the ritornello, building up the episodes, often into multipartite constructions, and using different tonalities in the episodes and (much more rarely) in the ritornellos. After anaylzing the suggested rondos, or any others, discuss the composer's ways and means of achieving a balance between unity and variety, and dare to express an opinion about his success in doing so. Remember that the demands both for unity and variety increase with the length of any piece of music.

SUGGESTED ASSIGNMENTS

1. The following are suggestions for analysis:
   Rondeau from Partita in C minor for harpsichord, Bach
   Rondo from Sonata in D (Urtext No. 37), Haydn
   Andante Cantabile from Sonata, Opus 13, Beethoven
   Alla Menuetto from Sonata, Opus 49, No. 2, Beethoven
   Für Elise, Beethoven
   Andante favori in F (Piano) (Var.), Beethoven
   (Notice especially the sectional construction of this piece, each part cadencing. The coda serves as a final return of the principal theme.)
   Rondo from Sonata, Opus 53, in D (Var.), Schubert
   Rondino (violin and piano), Beethoven-Kreisler
   Hungarian Dance No. 7, Brahms
   Symphony in C minor, Third Movement (Var.), Brahms
   Arabesque in C, Schumann
   Polonaise, Opus 53, Chopin
   Polonaise from Andante Spianato and Polonaise Brillante, Chopin
   "La Chasse" from *Six Etudes for Piano*, Paganini-Liszt
   Au Bord d'une Source (piano) (Var.), Liszt
   Sevilla (piano), Albeniz
   "Danse Russe" from *Petrouchka*, Stravinsky
   Pavane for a Dead Princess (Var.), Ravel

2. The student is warned that most of the rondos which appear as final movements in the piano sonatas of Beethoven, as well as many independent concert rondos, belong to the type known as the sonata-rondo and should be avoided until after a study of sonata-form Chapter 8.

   The use of rondo constructions in pieces that are not conventional rondos is an extremely interesting area for study. Probably it should not be emphasized at this point, but the following very familiar pieces should afford some hint of the possibilities.
   Nocturne, Opus 37, No. 2, Chopin
   Design: *A–B–A–B* (transposed)*–A–Codetta*
   Mazurka in B minor, Opus 33, No. 4, Chopin

   Design: $\|: A(24)\ A^2(24)\ B(16) :\|\ ^3\ \dfrac{C}{a(32)\ b(16)}\ T.(17)\ A(24)\ Coda(8)$

   Waltz in C-sharp minor, Opus 64, No. 2, Chopin
   Design: *A–B–C–B–A–B*. Part *B*, a sixteen-measure period with written out repeat, supplants Part *A* as the ritornello. This occurs also in the Waltz in A-flat, Opus 42.

3. Extravagant uses of the short ritornello may be found in Beethoven's Ecossaise in E-flat (see Example 6), and Schumann's *Faschingsschwank aus Wien*.

---

³ Repeat marks used only in the graph.

7

Theme With Variations

The practice of introducing variations into the playing or singing of a melody is certainly older than any known system of written notation. When songs and dance tunes were transmitted solely by ear, changes were bound to occur, but it is easy to believe that popular performers then, as now, indulged in such liberties as their imaginations suggested and their abilities permitted. We know that skill in musical variation was highly respected and cultivated in the Middle Ages, and that by the end of the sixteenth century the theme with variations had become an established means of achieving length in composition. It has remained so to the present day.

The variation form is not only the oldest among extended musical forms; it is also the simplest in concept and, finally, the most flexible. A set of variations can be fashioned to resemble almost any standard form. It can be of any desired length, that is, it can contain any number of variations. It may end with a fantasia or a fugue, or with a simple restatement of the original theme.

The length of the theme is a factor affecting the number of variations. A short one will permit a greater number without producing a wearisome overall length. For this reason, and the even more practical one, that the mind should be able to retain, at first hearing, an impression of the theme in its entirety, a single period of from eight to sixteen measures will be found most often.

DOUBLES

There is, however, a type of variation, rather peculiar to the baroque era, in which an extended multi-partite composition (such as a gavotte, bourrée, sarabande, and others) is repeated in an ornamented version. Such versions were called *doubles*, a French word meaning variations. Haydn's well-known Andante con variazioni in F minor belongs to this type. The theme itself is in two parts, the second in the parallel major key. Each of the parts is in binary form. The parts-graph for the theme alone is:

$$\overset{\textstyle A}{\overline{\|: a(12) :\|: b(17) :\|}} \qquad \overset{\textstyle B}{\overline{\|: a(10) :\|: b(10) :\|}}$$
$$\text{F minor} \qquad\qquad\quad \text{F major}$$

a total of ninety-eight measures with the repeats. The composer wisely confined himself to two variations. Incidentally, Part *A* is heard again in its original form just before the coda.[1]

---

[1] For other instructive examples of *doubles*, see Rameau's *Niais de Sologne* (actually a gavotte), Bach's English Suites 1 (Courante), 2 (Sarabande), 3 (Sarabande), and 6 (Sarabande). Smaller examples may be found in Couperin's First and Second *Ordres*.

It will help in the understanding of variational techniques before the nineteenth century (and, to some extent, during it) to recall that the art of improvisation was then in great popular favor. Improvisation and variations went hand in hand. Any player who set about improvising on a theme immediately began to treat his audience to a series of variations. His effectiveness depended on keeping the theme *perceptibly present*. This type of entertainment, which often was incredibly banal, influenced composers who took the pains to give their efforts permanent form on paper. Most of this music reflects the fashion of the time: it was written merely to ornament the melody, and was primarily exploited for virtuoso purposes.

This goes far to explain why early composers of variations seldom ventured beyond the melodic and harmonic horizons of the chosen theme. It could be festooned with arpeggios, rapid scales, trills, or broken chords, but there must be no bold changes of harmony or key nor wide departures from the prescribed melodic line.

The prevalent fashion among English composers late in the sixteenth century is fairly represented by Example 105, which shows a four-measure phrase in pavane style by Giles Farnaby and his manner of treating it in variations. In all there are twelve variations from which we quote three. The choice and order of harmonies remain the same throughout.

Example 105.   Farnaby, "Rosa Solis," *Fitzwilliam Collection*

This concentration on the melodic line and the correlative rarity of harmonic or structural changes continued, with a few brilliant exceptions, such as certain works by Bach, for about two hundred years, that is, until Beethoven.

Beethoven brought about an entirely new and immensely advanced conception of the variation. He and his successors often lead the listener so far from the theme that any direct similarity is almost completely obscured. These great masters used a theme as a point of departure. They composed not so much variations *on* a theme as variations *from* it. It would be truthful to say that their variations are, more often than not, metamorphoses of a theme.

It is impossible to analyze completely a work of genius. There are always mystical qualities which defy definition. Yet it is possible to isolate and catalog the major *mechanical* means used by the great writers of variations. The list below will give some idea of these techniques considered singly. In actual practice they are almost never used singly, but in combination. The possibility of variation in these combinations is infinite.

The major resources of the variation writer may be set down as follows:

1. Embellishments of the melodic line.
2. Changes in the melodic line with or without changes of harmony.
3. Changes of harmony with or without changes in the melodic line.
4. Passing modulations or digressions into other keys without dislodging the original tonic.
5. Change of key, that is, building the entire variation around a new tonic.
6. Change of mode.
7. Changes of rhythm. This includes use of polyrhythms.
8. Changes of tempo.
9. Changes of dynamics.
10. Changes of articulation, that is, *staccato* versus *legato*, etc. This may be expanded to include changes in phrasing and the placing of accents.
11. Changes of register.
12. Contrapuntal inversions, such as moving a melody from the soprano to the bass, in which case the accompaniment sounds above it. This is an expansion of No. 11.
13. The use of polyphony, that is, the addition of one or more melodies in counterpoint to the original one.
14. The use of canon, in which a theme is heard in counterpoint against itself, a refinement of No. 13.
15. The use of fugato. The so-called fugues (exclusive of final fugues) found in variations are usually fugatos, which are freer in structure and more adaptable to the limitations of a variation. (See Variation 5 in the final movement of Beethoven's Opus 109.)
16. Changes of timbre, that is, changes of instrumentation (band, orchestra or other instrumental groups) or of registration (organ).

One may also find some use of thematic fragmentation, which means that only a portion of the theme is the basis for an entire variation. (See Variation 4, p. 98.) Other common techniques such as diminution, augmentation, and so on, can often be effective.

If embellishment of the melodic line is the only element of variety, the change from the original is superficial. The fundamental structure of the piece remains as it was and little, if anything, has been added. The same may be said of small changes in harmony, articulation, or accompanimental patterns. On the other hand, changes of rhythm, modulations, substitutions of new themes, or themes introduced in counterpoint are real structural changes. As the art of variation writing progressed it became more and more a test of mastery over *structural* change.

Little ingenuity is required to ornament a melody. On the other hand, the achievement of total unity where every variation has an individuality of its own demands a special and rare talent. There have been few really great composers of variations, but there is general agreement that Brahms was one of these.

SECTIONALIZED VARIATIONS

Two of the finest productions by Johannes Brahms are used in this chapter to illustrate the sectionalized theme with variations and the passacaglia. Such a choice is made because these works serve our purpose ideally and are at the same time universally acclaimed masterpieces. Brahms was blessed with a powerful musical mind and sound common sense. He never mistook length for quality. He judged accurately the possibilities of a theme and, having chosen his material, held firmly to it. In no other music can one find a more illuminating use of the mechanics of variation writing.

The little air which Brahms uses as a theme in his Opus 24 was borrowed from a fellow German. It may be found in the first of three *Leçons* written by Handel for harpsichord. Handel himself wrote several variations on it. It is short, simple, forceful, and symmetrical. In form this theme is unipartite even though each phrase of the period is marked for repetition.

For reasons of space only the first four measures of each variation selected for study will be given. This should be sufficient to identify the techniques used. The harmonies should be noted and remembered. Even more important are the *critical* tones of the theme and their order. These appear on the staff below.

Melodically, Variation 1 is an embellishment of the theme. The harmonies are virtually unchanged. The distinctive features include:

More energetic rhythm.
Staccato, a change from *legato*.
Accents on the second half of the beat.
Movement in continuous sixteenths.
Increase in dynamics.

Var. 1

Variation 2 is also an embellished version of the theme. New harmonies attend short modulations (digressions) into nearly related keys: V^9–I of the supertonic (C minor) in measures 1 and 2, and V^7–I of the subdominant in measure 3. Also note:

Four-part counterpoint.
Much use of chromatic tones.
Polyrhythms (in this instance, 3 versus 2).
Movement in continuous triplet eighths.
Faster tempo.

Var. 2

From here on new melodies are constantly evolving and specific attention need seldom be called to them, except to cite structural links with the original theme. The change to a massive bravura style in Variation 4 provides a sharp contrast. The first three notes of the theme form a motive in diminution which dominates the variation. We also find:

Allusion to G minor.
Much use of staccato.
Offbeat accents.

Var. 4

Variation 5 is in the parallel or tonic minor. Beginning with the first *b*-flat in the right hand, observe the resemblance to the contour of the theme. Observe also that the sequence (measure 3 and 4) has been moved forward in the measure. This rhythmic shift accounts for the sixteenths (diminution) on the fourth beat, measure 2. Compare with measure 1.

The key scheme, tonic minor to its relative major (D-flat), occurs in several of the other variations such as the one which follows.

This variation and the preceding one are constructed on two contrapuntal lines with occasional harmonies filled out, but the return to *legato* and the reduced dynamics offer a strong contrast.

Var. 5

Variation 6 is a strict canon. The pitch interval is an octave, and the time interval is equal to a quarter of a measure. The melody grows out of the first three critical tones (see p. 96). To show how the composer proceeds with a canon in contrary motion, the first measure of the second part is included.

Variations 7 and 8 are closely related rhythmically. Both are dominated by the energetic recurrence of the figure ♩ ♪♪ . As unlikely as it may seem, the critical tones still play an important part.

Variation 8 is a lesson in double counterpoint. The two parts in the treble are inverted at the octave in measures 3 and 4. Similar inversions are continued throughout the variation.

The descending changes of register in Variation 10 are deceptive. If the melody had been held within a single octave it would have appeared as it does on the extra staff. Also note:

Mode alternating between major and minor.
Changing dynamics.

Variation 13 is unique in the set and musically one of the finest. It is in fact a short, slow movement. The key scheme, alternating between B-flat minor and D-flat major, has been found in several earlier variations. There is no change in the harmonic rhythm, I–V–I–IV | I–V–I. The new melody does not wander as far from the original contour as may be supposed at first glance. The general style, accentuated by the slow-paced accompaniment, is that of a *marche funèbre*, although there is no historical evidence that the composer considered it so. The mechanical differences from the theme and its setting by Handel (which the student should always keep in mind) affect melody, mode, key, harmonization (mostly parallel sixths), rhythm, and tempo.

Var. 13

Variation 20 is the most chromatic of the set. Also note:

Freer use of modulation than in any of the other variations.
Melody remaining close to the critical tones (try to trace them).
Movement in steady eighths and very legato.

Var. 20

Two measures only are given for the next two variations. A new tonic center (*g*) is set up in Variation 21, but the pitch of the critical tones remains as before. Note the polyrhythms (4 versus 3).

Variation 22 is a musette. Also note:

A return to the contours of the theme.
A return to B-flat major and the original harmonies.
Dotted note figures.

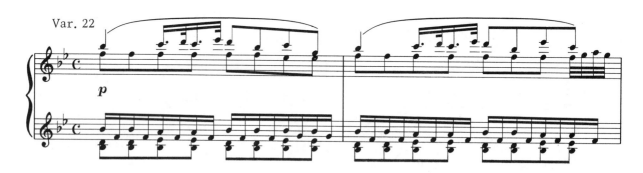

Variation 23 brings an abrupt contrast to the preceding two variations. Thematic bonds with the original air are difficult to discern. In this respect this is the most independent of the variations. Its twin (Variation 24, not shown) is but an elaboration of the same idea, actually a *double*.

The harmonic pattern is changed; the first measure, for example, is I–IV–VII⁷ (or incomplete V⁹). A common feature with Variation 22 is the pedal *b*-flat. Also note:

A mixture of modes injected by the minor subdominant.
Light staccato and very rapid tempo.

The final variation (Number 25) is in the bravura spirit of Variation 4 but with an even more driving rhythm. There is a new melody, yet at the same time, tonal and harmonic ties with the theme in its original setting are restored. The continuous sixteenths recall Variations 1 and 4.

Var. 25

The forces of contrast interact not only between the theme and the individual variations but between and among the variations themselves. No one understood this more instinctively than did Brahms, which means that he had a keen concern for the organization of the work as a whole. It should be noticed that the first twelve variations move in speeds of *moderato* to *allegro;* that the one true touch of *adagio* (Variation 13) is placed exactly in the center of the set; that Variations 14 through 19 (bearing such directives as *sciolto, più mosso, grazioso, leggiero e vivace*) convey something of the atmosphere of a scherzo; and that after Variation 22 the speed increases to the end. Also, notice that the three predominantly chromatic variations (2, 9, and 20) are spaced in a manner calculated to secure a maximum of contrast in a general diatonic background.

Although the subject of fugue is not taken up systematically until Chapter 11, the great fugue which brings this series of variations to a conclusion is excellent listening and not difficult to understand. The subject, based on the first five tones of Handel's theme, is heard several times in inversion and twice in augmentation. The texture of this fugue is not forbiddingly polyphonic and at times is positively homophonic. The closing chorale, accompanied by a motive derived from the subject of the fugue, is surely one of the most stirring moments in piano music.

The cursory study just made of excerpts from Brahms's Opus 24 should be supplemented by a thorough examination of the complete work. Many details worthy of notice are to be found in the second half of the variations which could not be given here. There are always good recordings of this music available, any one of which would add greatly to the interest and usefulness of this study.

It is evident throughout that the work is that of a disciplined mind. The theme was not used as an excuse to go flying in all directions, and Brahms's powers as a melodist and tonal architect were in constant play but always subordinated to the task at hand. These variations are therefore especially well suited for analysis and demonstration, which also is, or should be, a disciplined pursuit.

The use of the words "critical tones" should not mislead the student into believing that all variations are anchored to certain pitches in the theme. In some techniques, such as the reliance on a harmonic pattern, the theme may be completely disregarded. In such variations occurrences of the original tones are coincidental.

THE PASSACAGLIA AND THE CHACONNE

An undisputed generic distinction between these old dances, as we know them in baroque and later music, has never been established. A commonly accepted professional opinion is essentially this: a *passacaglia* (or *passacaille*) is a series of continuous variations over an ostinato bass, while a *chaconne* (or *ciacona*) is a series of continuous *harmonic* variations without such a bass. This conclusion is admittedly based on Bach's Passacaglia for Organ and Chaconne for Solo Violin. It would stand if Bach could settle the matter.

Unfortunately it leaves out of reckoning many other compositions by composers of good standing who did not conform. To cite a worthy exception: Handel wrote a chaconne (his own title) consisting of a short harmonized melody and sixty-two variations. The bass line placed under this melody is a familiar one often used as an ostinato. Handel retained it throughout the whole series and *always* in the bass. Even Bach, in his Passacaglia, moves the ostinato into the upper voices in three of the variations. If a ground bass is the mark of a passacaglia, then Handel, in this chaconne, has held more doggedly to the rule than did Bach.

The use of the term "variations" as applied to a passacaglia requires some qualification. In such a piece, the ground bass is itself the most important, and occasionally the only, unifying agent. There is no other theme making demands on the composer. He is free to write whatever melodies above the bass may suit him, and is bound only by the laws of common sense. These melodies may or may not be variations of anything. Small figural variants may be worked into the ostinato but these are of slight consequence against the parade of ever-new themes in the upper parts which naturally preempt attention. In a strict sense therefore a passacaglia may not be variations at all, but a series of free melodies or harmonic fantasies over a common bass.

If the variations are merely harmonic, as has been claimed for the chaconne, the composer is given a virtual *carte blanche*, for these harmonies are usually the common chords of the key and, again, a genuine program of "variations" may become exceedingly tentative, however great the music.

The ground or ostinato bass is a very old device in both vocal and instrumental music. As its popularity spread among composers certain patterns became more or less fixed and, in fact, became public property. These patterns were dictated not so much by custom as by the functions that such a bass must perform. An ostinato bass should, like the subject of a fugue, confirm the key at once. This explains why tonal ostinatos set up a solid tonic-dominant relationship. Almost all of them begin on the tonic, move diatonically or skip up or down to the dominant, and cadence on the tonic. Other tones of the scale will be heard along the way. All this must be accomplished in a few measures—the average ground is of four or eight measures. In a passacaglia or chaconne the meter is triple, but there are plenty of grounds in duple or *alla breve* meter.

The following example illustrates the points just made, especially the reference to the prevalence of certain patterns.

Purcell, Ground in Gamut

Purcell used the same line (with chromatic passing tones) in his famous Lament "When I am Laid in Earth," (*Dido and Aeneus*). Handel used it in his Chaconne. It appears in a contrapuntal disguise in the following ground by John Blow (1648–1708).

Since we will be focusing our attention in the next pages on the fourth movement of Brahms's Fourth Symphony, the ostinato used by Bach in the Chaconne of his Cantata, No. 150 ("Nach dir, Herr, verlanget mich") holds a special interest.

The appropriateness of this quotation as an introduction to Brahms's masterpiece must be instantly apparent to anyone who is familiar with the symphony. It is said that Brahms discussed the possibilities of this theme as a basis for a symphonic movement with his friend von Bulow. The story could well be true; the similarity of Brahms's theme with that of Bach is too close to be altogether coincidental. But again, it is another of those natural patterns, this one *ascending* to the dominant, so that we may be fairly sure that it was not original with either Bach or Brahms.

Some scholars flatly classify Brahms's composition as a chaconne while others as readily call it a passacaglia. The facts themselves are these: of the thirty-four variations, eleven are definitely built on an ostinato bass, twelve show the theme at the top in harmonized variations, and the others have the theme dispersed between parts, or in an inner voice, or only inferred. It is therefore neither completely a passacaglia nor a chaconne. In the author's experience most musicians, including conductors, have referred to it as a passacaglia, and so, for convenience, it will be called in this analysis.

Our piano reduction is only an approximation of the original score, as any transcription from an orchestral medium must ever be. It is intended as an instructional aid. All important thematic material is preserved, although it has occasionally been necessary to transpose it to a different octave to bring it within reach of the hand. Brahms did not number the variations, but we have done so to facilitate identification in class discussions.

Brahms presents his theme as a harmonized melody. The manner of harmonizing shows his originality. The first chord is the subdominant and in an inversion. The cadential dominant is altered to show an augmented sixth. The final chord has a major third which enhances the dramatic impact. Instrumentation of these measures is entirely woodwinds and brass.

Variation 1 (omitted) is a subdued repetition of the theme.

Variation 2 is the first of many beautiful and independent melodies Brahms introduces in counterpoint to the ostinato. The latter is inconspicuously sounded here in an inner part (low strings). Notice how naturally the melody flows over the cadence into Variation 3 where the ostinato becomes the basis of a melody resolutely given out by the woodwinds and brass. In the selective use of instrumentation this passacaglia may be likened to an orchestral concerto.

Variations 4 through 7 belong to a group. The ground bass is maintained throughout. Observe the similar endings of Variations 4 and 7 and how Variation 5 is melodically linked to Variation 6.

Var. 5

Var. 6

Var. 7

Variations 8 and 9 are twins. Both show a sequence in the relative major. The ostinato is shortened in both to seven measures with the eighth measure put in the subdominant.

Variation 10 is a play on dominant seventh chords. The tones of the ostinato are not always in the bass but do belong to the harmony.

Var. 10

Variation 11 is harmonically an elaboration of Variation 10. The final *b* in the bass should be understood as holding through to a resolution on the first beat of the next variation.

Var. 11

Variation 12 initiates a change in meter which in effect doubles the length of the ostinato. This variation together with the next three forms an Andante group. The flute solo grows directly out of the theme. Here and in certain other variations the notes of the basic theme are cued in as a guide.

Var. 12

Variation 13 brings a change to the major mode, which of course means a *g*-sharp in the ostinato. The critical tones are conspicuously placed in the dialogue between the clarinet and the oboe until we arrive at the fifth measure. Again there is a delayed resolution at the end.

Variations 14 and 15 are twins. The tones of the ostinato are retained in the harmonies though not always in the bass. In Variation 15 a line moves chromatically from the *e* up to *b*.

Variation 16 is a strong restatement of the theme, enlivened by the biting octave passage in the strings. The drop in the theme to the lower register does not occur in the orchestral score—it is done here for clearer performance on a keyboard.

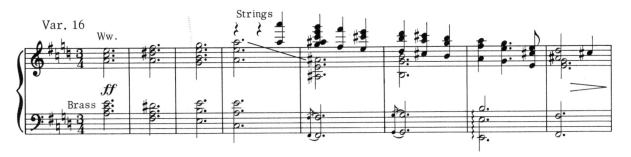

The string tremolo of Variations 17 and 18 cannot be satisfactorily transcribed to the piano. However, the thematic and harmonic structures are shown. The end of the theme has been altered in both variations.

Brahms's freedom in the matter of key, while clinging to the original pitch of the ostinato, is noteworthy. In the next two variations (twins) he moves from E minor through D major, G minor, B major back to E minor.

As in Variation 15 the chromatic element is stressed in Variation 21 from the tonic up to the dominant (fifth measure). From this point another and higher ascending line can be picked up: *d♯–e–f♯–g–g♯–a–* to *b*, the first note of Variation 22.

Var. 21

Variation 22 is a scherzo. The variations up to this point have followed without exception the rising contour of the theme. This variation is an exception, beginning at the highest tone and subsiding downward. See also Variations 27 and 28.

Var. 22

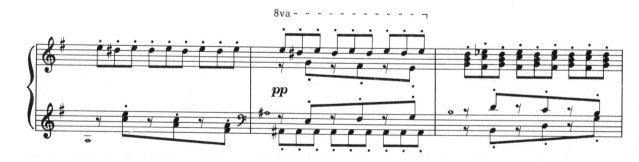

Variation 23 is a continuation of Variation 22, building to a climax in measure 6.

Variation 24 (omitted) serves as a restatement of the theme. It sets off a sort of recapitulation. Compare Variations 25 and 26 with Variations 2 and 3.

Variations 27 and 28 begin in C, move through G back to E minor. The *a*-sharp is not sounded in the fifth measure of Variation 27, nor inferred in the harmony. This measure is unique among "fifth" measures in these variations. The final *a* in the cello figure (measure 5) could logically have been sharped, although repeated hearings are convincing that Brahms was right in choosing a literal repetition of the figure in measure 4.

Variations 29 and 30 form a final pair. There is no relaxing of fidelity to the basic theme in either. Discuss the use of the ostinato in Variation 29. Have any of the tones been omitted? Shifted? Augmented or diminished, actually or by inference?

The double row of octaves in Variation 30 is especially interesting as it forms a close canon. For the first time there is an extension, this one of four measures leading into the coda.

The coda is presented without comment. The student should be able to locate four variations within these final measures and explain all special features.

A general survey of Brahms's Passacaglia shows that it breaks down into four divisions or groups, not including the coda.

1. Variations 1 through 11, a series in moderate tempo in which the theme is used, with two exceptions, as a ground bass.
2. Variations 12 through 15, corresponding to a slow movement.
3. Variations 16 through 23, the most energetic variations. We have likened Variation 22 to a scherzo. Variations 19, 20, and 21 have somewhat the same spirit.
4. Variations 24 through 30, a fourth group, containing a very clear recapitulation.

This passacaglia and the variations on Handel's theme show a somewhat similar grouping. This end-to-end perspective of extended sets of variations is very important and should receive serious study. No matter how varied and intriguing the individual items in the chain may be, the composer cannot ignore the power and effect of these major divisions.

An approach to the sonata sequence of moods may be seen in many variations written since early classical years; that is, a first group in *moderato* to *allegro* speed, a slower middle group (often with a change of mode), and a final group in rapid tempo. César Franck carried out this plan so strongly in his *Variations symphoniques* (see Chapter 12) that the groups are often referred to as movements.

Beethoven's famous *Thirty-two Variations in C minor* offers a profitable study in both the use of techniques and total organization. These variations could (with excellent reason) have been published as a chaconne, since they are based on an eight-measure theme (see Example 66) and are played without pause.

SUGGESTED ASSIGNMENTS

1. Rachmaninoff's *Rhapsody on a Theme of Paganini*, Opus 43,[2] for piano and orchestra is one of the most important works in variation form to appear in the twentieth century. This theme in its entirety may be seen in Example 75. In this assignment, the first phrase (four measures) of the theme and the equivalent in eight of the variations are quoted. With our table of techniques presented earlier in the chapter in mind, analyze the techniques used. Note that the corresponding passage in some of the variations may extend beyond four measures.

   Rachmaninoff consistently repeats both parts of the binary form. By varying the repetitions he writes variations within variations. In this enlarged frame we find fantasias that range far from the simple lines and proportions of the original melody. However, the identifications should not be difficult in the passages quoted. Give special attention to details of similarity.

2. Before analyzing the excerpt from Variation 18, write in D-flat a version of the original first four measures of the theme. Adapt it to 3/4 meter and compare with Rachmaninoff's melody. Did he lose himself in a sentimental moment, or is the variation solidly based on a valid thematic inference?

[2] Excerpts by permission of Charles Foley, Inc., copyright owners.

Var. 24

3. Detailed studies, in the manner adopted earlier in this chapter, should be made of other sets of variations. Suitable material will be found in the following list:

First movement (Variations), Sonata, Opus 26, Beethoven

Variations on an Original Theme, Opus 34, Beethoven

(Notice the unusual key scheme of this work.)

Impromptu (Variations), Opus 142, No. 3, Schubert

Variations Sérieuses, Mendelssohn

First Movement, Sonata, K. 331, Mozart

More advanced:

Variations on a Theme by Haydn (Orchestra), Brahms

4. Write at least two variations on the following theme with definite techniques in mind. Original harmonies given. Or, invent a theme of your own and do the same.

Adapted from Purcell

5. Study:

Passacaglia in C minor for Organ, Bach

Finale from *Variations on a Theme by Haydn* (For orchestra or two pianos), Brahms

6. Bach's Chaconne for Solo Violin (Second Partita) should be reviewed as an example of variations based on a harmonic rather than a thematic background. No ground bass is involved. Study the "group" organization of this work, the change of mode in the slow middle variations, and how the great effects are prepared in advance over several variations. It has been transcribed for piano by Busoni and for orchestra by Stokowski.

7. If any of the short grounds of Henry Purcell are available, they should be played in class for purposes of comparison.

8. The following works are relatively recent:

Passacaglia (for piano), Copland (Salabert)

Passacaglia for Piano, Piston (Mercury)

Passacaglia for Orchestra, Webern (Universal)

These works contain some transposition of theme and very free variations.

8

The Sonata-Form

The term "sonata" has been used in music since the middle years of the sixteenth century. At one time it seems to have been applied to almost anything written exclusively for instruments. As a result of this long and complicated history, sonatas appear on musical programs in a variety of forms. A modern audience may find itself listening to any of the following:

A sonata da camera by Corelli, differing little, if at all, from a dance suite.
A trio-sonata by Purcell, scored for violins, viola da gamba, and harpsichord in four or five movements (non-dance types).
A sonata for unaccompanied violin by J. S. Bach in four movements, of which the second is a fugue.
A sonata for harpsichord (piano) by Domenico Scarlatti in one movement in binary form.
A sonata by Liszt in one movement, resembling a fantasia.
A sonata by Mozart in three movements, comprising a set of variations, a minuet, and a hybrid allegretto.

Even after this brief list it is obvious that the word "sonata" is meaningless as to form. However, if we say "sonata-form," certain definite information is conveyed as to the overall construction of a movement and the distribution and treatment of themes. Although the word "sonata-form" is not ideal, since other forms are found just as often in the movements of a sonata, no better term is at hand and this one has a wide acceptance based on a common understanding.

Even less satisfactory are such limited inventions as "first-movement form," or "sonata-allegro form." It frequently happens that a first movement is *not* in sonata-form (See Beethoven's Opus 26; Opus 27, No. 1; or Mozart's K. 331.) Add to this the fact that many later movements *are* in this form; for example, see Beethoven's Opus 2, No. 1; Opus 27, No. 2; Opus 31, No. 2; or Mozart's Symphony in C (*Jupiter*), in all of which the *last* movement is in sonata-form. Three of the four movements of Mozart's Symphony in G minor, No. 48, are in sonata-form.

The term "sonata-allegro" is equally misleading, for tempo is not a decisive factor. The most that can be said for these impractical labels is that they have a certain statistical support based on the fact that most movements in sonata-form are first movements and are played at speeds of *moderato* or faster.

THE SOLO SONATA

Since baroque times the word "sonata" has become restricted by custom to compositions for a solo instrument (piano, organ, violin, cello, and others) or two instruments in duo, such as two pianos or piano with violin or cello. Such usage has nothing basically to do with form. The sonata-form, the most important in music, is equally present in the symphony (a sonata for orchestra), the concerto (a sonata for solo instrument with orchestra), or the trio, quartet, quintet, sextet, etc. (a sonata arranged for any of these combinations).

124

In its fully developed state sonata-form is a ternary formation. Its three parts are known as the *exposition (A)*, *development (B)*, and *recapitulation* or *reprise (A²)*. To these may be added an *introduction* and a *coda*.

Exposition.

An exposition may contain as few as two simple themes—a primary and a subordinate one. The primary theme will be in the tonic while the subordinate theme will be in another (usually closely related) key. In the more than two centuries since the sonata-form became a standard fixture, the preference of composers has been to put the subordinate theme, *as heard in the exposition,* in the relative major if the primary theme is in minor, and in the dominant if the primary theme is in major. Needless to say, there have been frequent deviations from this classical practice, some of which will be seen later in this chapter.

These key relationships did not originate with the sonata-form. They came into common use along with the emergence of the early binary form, during which time man's growing consciousness of harmonic functions reached certain conclusions which affected all subsequent tonal composition.

In early sonatas and symphonies the subordinate theme was often a variant of the primary theme. (See Example 112.) But the attractive possibilities of contrasting themes were eventually realized. Once established, this element of thematic contrast remained a permanent feature of sonata-form.

Beethoven was especially happy in his ability to create striking first themes which at once arrest attention and establish a key.[1] More often than not these initial ideas are brief. Invariably the subordinate portion of the exposition is of greater length than the primary theme.[2] The subordinate ("subordinate" being relevant only to the order in which themes are presented and in no sense implying inferiority) theme is very frequently of a more subdued and lyric quality, a natural reaction to the aggressive energy of many first themes. This is ideally illustrated in Beethoven's Fifth Symphony.

If the exposition is terminated by a melodic idea distinct from the preceding subordinate theme, then we have what is frequently called a closing theme. The name defines it. The classical closing theme evolved through the inclination of many eighteenth-century composers to spin out the cadence formula at the end of a movement. This swinging back and forth between tonic and dominant harmonies usually produced nothing more than a perfunctory coda. Later and more imaginative composers, especially Beethoven, built up this final part, assigning to it a real thematic importance in the sonata scheme. One eventual result was the enrichment of the subordinate theme by the addition of another part which no longer functioned strictly as a closing theme since it in turn came to be followed by a coda.

It is probably true that most closing themes, even as a final part of a multi-part subordinate theme, have a perceptible subsiding quality, but the reverse is frequently true when we find instead a quickening of the action (See Chopin's Sonata in B-flat minor or Beethoven's Opus 53 and Opus 57.) If a closing theme is followed by a coda, in particular a coda of some pretension, this author prefers to incorporate the closing theme as a part within the subordinate theme.

Development.

The second major division of the sonata-form may be appropriately called a development only to the extent that materials from the preceding exposition are actually developed. Even the greatest masters would often introduce new ideas during its course. In certain sonatas, such as Mozart's K. 332, an entirely new theme dominates this section. In such cases it is more accurate to refer to it as the *middle theme.*

---

[1] The claim that the formal function of a primary theme is to establish a key is not without some foundation in fact, even though it is a bit of an overstatement. Activity in tonal music should, and generally does, start from a firm tonal base. At times Beethoven did not wait for the theme but sounded the tonic chord at once. (See Symphonies 2, 3, and 7.)

[2] By "subordinate portion" is meant everything in the exposition after the formal close of the primary theme.

However, development is the rule and nowhere in music in this form can the genius of a great composer be more brilliantly evidenced. The developments of Beethoven's Opus 57 (*Appassionata* Piano Sonata), his Third and Fifth Symphonies, or any of the four symphonies of Brahms, stand as superlative examples.

Unlike the exposition and recapitulation, there are no traditional rules of form in writing a development, for it consists of an optional number of sections of any desired length. Sharp cadential separations are rather uncommon, either between the sections or at the end. The sections are distinguished more by their content, each being devoted to the exploitation of a particular motive or idea, or combination of ideas.

Nor are there any rules about what is to be extracted from the exposition for development. The composer can choose what he will from any of the announced themes—this includes transitions, codettas, or even an introduction. The techniques he will use are in some respects the same as those we have seen in the writing of variations, although the emphasis is now on details of a theme rather than on the entire theme.

Most frequently found are:

Thematic fragmentation (probably combined with sequence). Themes, especially opening themes, used in sonatas and sonata countertypes, i.e., the symphony and others, are often dependent on some striking figuration which lends itself naturally to repetitive and motivic treatment in various ways. This means that only a part of a theme may be used.

Modulation. There are no restrictions of key in development. Frequent changes of tonal center and harmonic patterns are to be expected. This is one of the most effective sources of contrast to the more or less prolonged key associations of the exposition.

Counterpoint. The use of two or more melodic lines running concurrently opens the way to every resource of counterpoint. Of these the most important are imitation, strict or free, and contrapuntal inversions (p. 133).

Other techniques of variation, such as augmentation, diminution, and thematic or figural inversions are of course to be met with from time to time.

Recapitulation.

The recapitulation follows closely the thematic order of the exposition. Certain modifications may be necessary to allow the subordinate parts to be heard in the tonic key. Also the various parts may be lengthened or compressed.

The final coda may be extended. In sonatas and symphonies conceived on a large scale the coda may appear as a major or fourth division of the movement, displaying, in all likelihood, the characteristics of a second development.

Transitions, or bridge passages, are important to sonata-form. Themes or their parts may or may not fully cadence. If they do not, a transition will likely be the means of progressing to the next theme. Such passages are not always merely functional but may contain inspirations of a high order, attaining the status of an episode. In other instances a transition may display the characteristics of a small development (See Example 109.)

Before proceeding to a general outline of sonata-form some clarification of common musical terms may be useful. *Theme* and *subject* are found in analytical writing without uniformity of meaning. The theme (subject) of a fugue may consist of a few notes, whereas a theme of a movement in sonata-form may include a succession of different and distinct melodies. The word "subject" is sometimes used in the same way.

In our outline, and in the analyses which follow, "theme" is used in an inclusive sense to cover, as circumstances require, one or several melodies. Each melody will be called a *part*. The divisions of a development will be called *sections*, since they are less affected by cadences and display less independence.

A workable outline of sonata-form is assembled as follows:

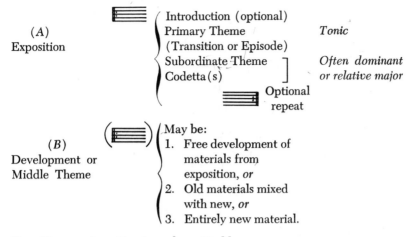

(A)
Exposition

Introduction (optional)
Primary Theme   *Tonic*
(Transition or Episode)
Subordinate Theme   *Often dominant*
Codetta(s)   *or relative major*
                            Optional
                            repeat

(B)
Development or
Middle Theme

May be:
1. Free development of
   materials from
   exposition, *or*
2. Old materials mixed
   with new, *or*
3. Entirely new material.

Transition or retransition is rarely omitted here.

(A²)
Recapitulation

Primary Theme   *Tonic* (usually)
(Transition or Episode)
Subordinate Theme   *Tonic*
Coda (possibly divided
into Codettas)   *Tonic* (▓▓)³

In Beethoven's Sonata Opus 14, No. 2 we find all the essential and characteristic features of the sonata-form within a movement of modest length. The exposition is quoted in its entirety.⁴

Beethoven leaves no doubt as to his intentions when he introduces the subordinate theme through its own dominant, measures 19–25. In less clear-cut cases, a reliable way to determine where and what the subordinate theme is is to study key relationships between analogous passages in the exposition and the recapitulation. At that point in the exposition where the dominant or other secondary key is answered by the tonic in the recapitulation, it is reasonably safe to assume that the subordinate theme has arrived or immediate preparation is being made for it.

The development sections of this sonata should be played slowly and carefully analyzed as to the sources of all thematic materials and the techniques used. The graph below should assist the student in identifying the three sections of this development.

The recapitulation of Beethoven's Opus 14, No. 2, is a literal repetition of the exposition until measure 138. At that point the music is transposed up a fourth to C major, which soon gives way to D major (established in measure 148), the dominant of G. In the process Part II of the primary theme is extended by three measures. For melodic reasons Part II of the subordinate theme is extended by two measures.

The motivic construction of the first part of the primary theme will surely be noticed. Even this short motive undergoes fragmentation in the coda at the end of the movement.

---

³ The joint repeat of development and recapitulation is characteristic of early works and may be explained as a vestige of the binary ancestry of sonata-form. Both Haydn and Mozart dropped it in their later symphonies. It occurs in none of Beethoven's symphonies and in only five of his thirty-two sonatas, including, curiously, two relatively late works, Sonatas Opus 78 and 79. The increasing length of sonatas and symphonies rendered such repetitions onerous, while the spontaneity intended in a good development raised an aesthetic objection to them.

⁴ It is assumed that the student will have access to complete copies of all the Beethoven sonatas.

Example 106. Beethoven, Sonata, Opus 14, No. 2, First Movement

In the preparation of sonata-form graphs the following abbreviations are used:

Pr. Th.—Primary Theme
Sub. Th.—Subordinate Theme
Br.—Bridge

T.—Transition
Ret.—Retransition
Ep.—Episode

C'ta.—Codetta
Mod.—Modulating
→ — Not fully cadenced.

Principal keys only are indicated here and there below the parts by capital letters. Numerals in brackets are measure totals—*per part, not by phrases.* If a part breaks down into two or more obvious measure groups, the measure count may be divided accordingly in certain instances. A complete breakdown by phrases is foregone in these graphs for space reasons. However, such graphs are to be encouraged on the part of students. Review the note on Page 76 concerning overlapping phrases.

Beethoven, Sonata Opus 14, No. 2, First Movement

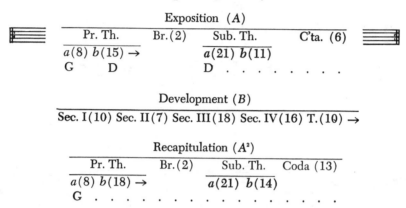

Exposition (A)

Pr. Th.	Br.(2)	Sub. Th.	C'ta. (6)
a(8) b(15) →		a(21) b(11)	
G	D	D	

Development (B)

Sec. I(10) Sec. II(7) Sec. III(18) Sec. IV(16) T.(10) →

Recapitulation (A²)

Pr. Th.	Br.(2)	Sub. Th.	Coda (13)
a(8) b(18) →		a(21) b(14)	
G			

Beethoven's Opus 2, No. 3, is richer in detail and thematic variety than the work just considered, but the basic features of sonata-form are just as clearly present. The outline below is given with a minimum of direct quotation and is intended as a model for the student to follow in making his own analyses of other movements in sonata-form.

Example 107. Beethoven, Sonata, Opus 2, No. 3, First Movement

Exposition (A)

Primary Theme, C Major

Part I (1-12)

etc.

Part II (13-20)

etc.

Part III (21-26)
Ending

Part II above is used twice later in the movement, but is replaced by other material as Part II, primary theme, in the recapitulation.

Episode (27–46). These twenty measures are not only transitional but meet the classic conditions of an episode as used in the homophonic forms. The thematic material is strong and is peculiar to this passage, which is repeated in the recapitulation. At the same time there is constant modulation.[6] The tonal center of gravity is G, but there are short digressions through C minor, D minor, and A minor, before settling on D major, which immediately functions as the dominant of G major, the key of the subordinate theme.

The episode is in two sections.

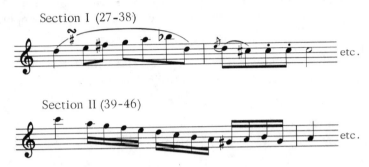

Subordinate Theme, G Major

Part I (47–60)

Part II (61–77) is an adaptation of primary Part II, an unusual occurrence. Measures 69–77 should be analyzed as an extension of Part II.

Codetta (78–90). Based on the motive

The final flourish in broken octaves and the repetition of the cadence (85–90) extend the closing phrase to nine measures.

Development (B) (91–138)

The derivative materials are taken from the codetta (see motive above) and the first measure of the primary theme. The motive

[6] The late and distinguished composer, Ernst von Dohnanyi, in addressing a class at Ohio University, said, "As long as the composer is modulating, the second (subordinate) theme has not arrived." As the speaker well knew, this statement would find its exceptions. But it is enough of a rule to be stated as such.

is the result of fragmentation and is prominent not only here but in the cadenza and the final codetta.

At measure 97 Beethoven begins an improvisational passage of twelve measures consisting of arpeggiated chords. This must be classified as new material. The passage is held together by the chromatic bass which moves from *b*-flat up to *d* (measure 109) where the opening measures of the primary theme give an impression, momentarily, of a recapitulation. This is quickly dispelled in a sequence of motivic figures, but the inclusion of the primary theme does serve to divide the development into two definite sections.

The transition (measures 129–138) is a further study in imitation and fragmentation.

Recapitulation (A²)

Primary Theme, C Major. Part I (139–146) is like that in the exposition.

Part II (147–154) is a substitution. The octave figure in the bass (measures 147–148 et seq.) is reminiscent of the extension to Part II of the subordinate theme (see measures 69–71). Beethoven's fondness for contrapuntal inversions is seen here: measures 149–150 are inverted in measures 151–152.[7]

Part III (155–160) is as found in the exposition.

Episode (161–180). This is transposed up a fourth or down a fifth.

Subordinate Theme, C Major (181–211). Both parts follow the pattern of the exposition.

Codetta, C Major (212–232). Extended by a series of arpeggiated diminished-seventh chords. The pause on the tonic six-four chord (measure 232) is a novelty in a sonata but routine in the classical solo concerto where it was used, as here, to set the stage for a cadenza. The parallel is continued in the trill over the dominant-seventh signalling the end of the cadenza. The cadenza itself grows from the primary motive.

Coda, C Major (233–257). Recalls the primary theme and the closing measures of the exposition.

Beethoven, Sonata, Opus 2, No. 3, First Movement

Exposition (A)			
Pr. Th.	Ep.	Sub. Th.	C'ta. (13)
$a(12)$ $b(8)$ $c(6)$ →	$a(12)$ $b(8)$ →	$a(14)$ → $b(8+9)$	
C	Mod.	G	

Development (B)	
Sec. I $(6+12)$ → Sec. II (20)	→ T. (10) →

Recapitulation (A²)			
Pr. Th.	Ep.	Sub. Th.	C'ta. (21) →
$a(8)$ $b(8)$ $c(6)$ →	$a(12)$ $b(8)$ →	$a(14)$ $b(8+9)$	
C		C	

Cadenza → Coda $(16+9)$

[7] Notice also the contrapuntal inversion in the subordinate theme.

Example 108.   Beethoven, Sonata, Opus 10, No. 3, First Movement

This movement offers another valuable lesson in the art of unification through the use of a short motive obtained by fragmentation. Other matters of special interest are the long succession of parts in the subordinate theme, in contrast to the brief primary theme; the use of transition at the end of the exposition, either to return to the beginning or proceed to the development; and the introduction of a new theme in the latter.

Exposition (A)

Primary Theme, D Major

The first four notes of this theme are the source of a motive (identified as the primary motive) which is used liberally elsewhere in the movement.

Measures 17–22 form a short transition in the nature of an introduction to the subordinate theme.

Subordinate Theme. Part I (23–30) begins, contrary to usual practice, in the relative minor, but cadences in F-sharp minor.

Part II (31–53) modulates to the dominant, A major.

Part III (54–93) is a union of two motivic passages, the first beginning:

and the second, at measure 67, involving the primary motive and a third (new) motive:

Primary Motive

The four-note primary motive is heard in the bass in measures 67–68. In the following measures (not given here) it is subjected to intensive development by sequence and inversion through several keys.

Part IV (Concluding) (94-105)

Codetta (106-113)

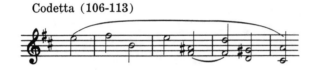

Transition. This is considered measures 114–124, if one is repeating the exposition, 114–132, if proceeding to the development. The entire transition is built on the primary motive.

Development (B)

Section I (133–140) is a bold new melody in B-flat heard at the outset. It is only a two-phrase period, and no further allusion is made to it.

ffp

Section II (141–157) contains a cadence in G minor in measure 149 and another in E-flat in measure 157. Measures 150–157 are a restatement of measures 142–149 and belong therefore to the same section.

Section III (158–183) is almost entirely transitional, gathering itself around the tone *d*. The word "retransition" is appropriate here. It means a leading *back* to a theme after a previous transition has led *away* from it.

This is not one of Beethoven's most distinguished efforts in development. Except for the ascending figures in the bass, consisting only of the successive tones of triads with their *appoggiaturi*, there is no kinship to previous themes, and even here the slight similarity to the opening phrase may be coincidental. This whole division could with much reason be classed as a middle theme rather than a development.

Recapitulation (A²)

This is regular except for local adjustments necessary to accommodate the changes of key. The primary theme comes to a full close in B, the dominant of E minor. Compare with the exposition. Part I of the subordinate theme now enters in E minor. The relation of E minor to the tonic (D major) as heard here is the same as B minor to the dominant as heard in the exposition.

The first codetta (287–298) is extended to twelve measures, modulating to G major. The measures which follow are another play on the primary motive. However, the passage here is not transitional as in the exposition, but a second codetta (299–327) ending in a full cadence (measure 327). The primary motive persists in the third and final codetta (328–343):

Beethoven, Sonata, Opus 10, No. 3, First Movement

	Exposition (A)		
Pr. Th. (16) T.(6)	Sub. Th.	C'ta.(8) T(11)	
	a(8) b(23) c(13+27) d(12)		
D	B minor F# minor A	A	

	Development (B) (Middle Theme)	
T.(18)	Sec. I(8) Sec. II(16) Sec. III(27) →	

	Recapitulation (A²)	
Pr. Th. (21)	Sub. Th.	C'ta. I(12)
	a(8) b(21) c(14+27) d(12)	
D	E minor B Minor D	

C'ta. II(29) C'ta. III(16)
D D

Only the first codetta can properly be included in the recapitulation. Consult a copy of the sonata.

Example 109. Mozart, String Quintet in D, K. 593, First Movement[8]

This quintet is not only great music but a remarkable example of Mozart's imagination in the use of sonata-form. It was written in 1790, a year before the composer died. As in his other quintets for strings, there are two viola parts.

Attention will be called to unusual formal features as they appear. The first such feature is immediately evident. There is a slow introduction, the only one of Mozart's string quintets to open in this fashion.

Introduction (21)

The primary theme[9] is made up of seven short ideas, all of which are much used later. In the order of performance these are: the march-like motive (22–23), the off-beat accented chords (V-I of the supertonic, 24–25), the scale in triplets (26–27), the six open chords at the cadence (28–29), and the three motives in measures 30–33. These last measures form a small codetta but they are so bound to the primary theme as to be a part of it. After a repetition of the primary theme, the little codetta is heard again, this time in the dominant (42–45) which sets the basic key for the remainder of the exposition.

Exposition

Primary Theme (22–45). This theme is in two parts as indicated.

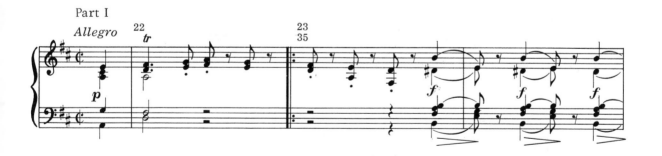

---

[8] All quotations in this example are, with one exception, reduced to two staves to facilitate demonstration at a keyboard.

[9] In preparing this primary theme for publication here, the author has indicated a first and second ending to save space. Bear this in mind in counting measures. The first measure of the primary theme is numbered 22.

Transition (46–62). This passage is analyzed as a transition more because of its position than its musical impact. Unlike most transitions, it ends in a full ·cadence (61–62). It could be called an episode, but episodes should stand melodically independent of other parts of a movement. In the present instance all the melodic material (three motives) is borrowed from the previous theme. Thus in reality this passage is a small development section interposed between the primary and the subordinate themes.

Subordinate Theme. There are three subordinate parts including a short closing theme. The first, surprisingly enough, begins with a canonic treatment of the first segment of the primary theme. This segment is heard again, in the cello, after an allusion to the characteristic accented chords of measures 24 and 25 in the upper strings. There is a full cadence in measure 75 but it is almost nullified by the active figure taken up simultaneously by the cello.

Subordinate Theme II is new material. Again there is a full cadence (measure 89) and again no halting as the closing theme moves in at once. The entire subordinate portion of this exposition is given below.

Part III (Closing Theme)

Bridge

Development

The development of Mozart's quintet is based entirely on four ideas presented in the primary theme. It is therefore a genuine development. One finds here a generous use of fragmentation, modulation to "foreign" keys, and imitation in counterpoint. There are two sections.

Section I (102–122) begins, after three measures of modulation, in the key of F major. Sixteen measures later it ends in a cadence in C-sharp major. It is developed exclusively from the first four measures of the primary theme.

Section II (123–143) is a commentary on the second half of the primary theme from which are quoted five measures only.

Recapitulation

Only Part I of the primary theme is heard in the recapitulation. Part II, in the exposition, is a literal repetition except for the modulation to the dominant. Since the cadence of Part I is in the tonic there is no reason for the repetition here. Such abbreviations of the recapitulation are to be observed frequently.[10]

The transition following the primary theme (157–188) must have fascinated Mozart. It is expanded to thirty-two measures, almost double its length in the exposition and only six measures shorter than the formal development. All the principal techniques of development are used again—fragmentation, sequence, modulation, and counterpoint.

There are unessential changes in Parts II and III of the subordinate theme resulting in additional measures. The greatest surprise of all is the return, after the recapitulation, of the introductory theme in its entirety with but slight modification. This is followed by a literal repetition of the primary theme as a coda. We have a sort of re-recapitulation, including the introduction itself, serving as a finale. The joint repeat of the development and recapitulation is indicated in the graph below.

[10] See also Brahms's Symphonies 2 and 3.

Mozart, Quintet, K. 593, First Movement

Introduction (21)
D

Exposition (A)

Pr. Th.	T.(13+5)	Sub. Th.	T.(5) →
$a(8+4)$ $a^2(8+4)$		$a(11)$ $b(14)$ $c(8)$	
D A	Mod.	A	

Development (B)

Sec. I (4+17) Sec. II (22) →
F   C# F# minor Mod.

Recapitulation (A²)

Pr. Th. (8+4) T.(32)	Sub. Th.	T.(5) →
D	$a(11)$ $b(16)$ $c(12)$	
	D	

Intro. Th. (19)   Coda (Pr. Th.) (8)
D   D

Numerous variations or modifications of the much-used sonata-form have inevitably occurred. We have already seen the freedom possible even when adhering to the basic classical design. Recall the disparity of length between the primary and secondary themes in Example 108, the introduction of developmental passages as transitions within the exposition in Example 109, the substitution of a new theme in the recapitulation in Example 107, the reappearance of an entire introduction *after* the recapitulation, and the repetition of a primary theme as coda in Example 109.

Yet, in all the examples just mentioned all the essential parts of sonata-form are present and in their normal order. The next two examples (graphs) are of movements in which this is not true.

The reversed position of the primary and subordinate themes in the recapitulation, Example 110, also favored by some modern composers, is known as the "arch" design. A lesser point of interest is the reappearance of the final measures of the primary theme at the end of the development, which comes to a full cadence. The recapitulation enters at once without transition.

Example 110. Mozart, Sonata, K. 311, First Movement

Exposition (A)   Development (B)

Pr. Th. (16)	Sub. Th.	Sec. I (16) Br. (2) Sec. II (21)
D	$a(8)$ $b(8+8)$	
	A	

Recapitulation (A²)

Sub. Th.	Pr. Th. (14)
$a(8)$ $b(4+8)$	
D	D

In Example 111, the primary theme is omitted in the recapitulation. The probable reason, as one may suspect on examining the music, is that the strongly motivic first theme so completely dominates the development that its repetition in the recapitulation would have been redundant.[11]

---

[11] For similar omissions see Chopin's Sonata in B minor and Beethoven's Sonata, Opus 31, No. 2. Sibelius habitually used the abbreviated recapitulation. See his First Symphony (first and fourth movements) and Fourth Symphony (first movement), which appears in Example 117.

Example 111. Chopin, Sonata in B-Flat Minor, Opus 35, First Movement

Introduction (4)

Exposition (A)

Pr. Th. (4+32) → Sub. Th. (16+24) → Cl. Th. (24) →
B♭ minor   D♭ . . . . .Mod.

Development (B)
Sec. I (32) Sec. II (16)   T. (16)

Recapitulation (A²)
Sub. Th. (40)   Cl. Th. (20) →   Coda (13)
B♭   B♭

SONATA-FORM IN THE SYMPHONY

The rise of the symphony as a standard form for orchestra closely paralleled the development of kindred forms for solo instruments and chamber groups. This was not a matter of chance since the foremost composers of the eighteenth and early nineteenth centuries were, almost without exception, active in all those areas where the sonata-form has proved to be most useful and enduring.

From its earliest days the symphony has been conceived on a somewhat broader scale than contemporary sonatas. This means an expanded and more elaborate treatment of sonata-form. Yet, in spite of the individual styles of composers and the changing tastes of the public, there has been, with few notable exceptions, general agreement in preserving the essential procedures of the classical design.

Our first two examples are taken from works of moderate length and exceptional clarity. The student will have gained sufficient familiarity with sonata-form to accept these examples as partially completed assignments to be checked and fully analyzed with an open score.

Example 112. Haydn, Symphony No. 104, (London No. 7), First Movement

In keeping with Haydn's custom this symphony begins with a slow introduction. The close similarity of the primary and subordinate themes shows his disposition to cling to this old means of securing unity, even in 1795, years after Mozart had proved it was unnecessary.

Exposition

Primary Theme, D Major

Subordinate Theme, A Major. Part I is substantially the same as Part I of the primary theme.

Codetta I

Codetta II

The development is in four sections (excluding the retransition). The cadences are of varying intensities. The primary motive is used in every section except the third. What is the source of the material in Section III?

This is a genuine development throughout. Analyze it thoroughly. Notice the abbreviated Part I of the subordinate theme in the recapitulation, also the greatly expanded Part II of the primary theme.

Measure totals are purposely omitted in the brackets of the next two graphs. The student should supply these after investigating the scores.

Haydn, Symphony 104, *(London No. 7)*, First Movement

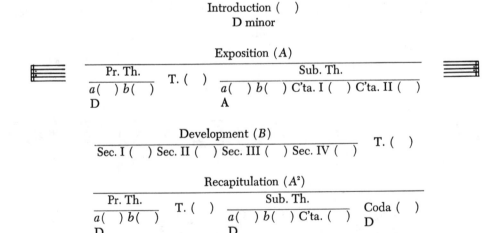

Example 113.   Schubert, Symphony No. 5, First Movement

The primary theme can be divided into three parts (i.e., 14+6+16). However, the six measures (19–24) offer nothing more than a four-measure play (by melodic inversion) on the opening motive, plus two measures whose sole function is to lead into the next part. There is no cadence in measure 18. In the author's opinion, the passage is more logically explained and heard as an extension to Part I.

Exposition

Introduction (1–4)
Primary Theme, B-Flat Major

Part II is a modified repetition of Part I.

Transition. This is strong enough to be considered an episode. Notice how it springs from the primary motive.

Subordinate Theme, F Major

Codetta I

Codetta II

Development

This is in two sections and entirely derived from previous materials. The eighth-note runs in Section I are patterned on measures 3 and 4 of the introduction.

Recapitulation

The primary theme returns in the key of the subdominant (E-flat). This change from the usual practice preserves the original key relationship of the two principal themes—tonic-dominant is answered by subdominant-tonic.[12] Otherwise the recapitulation is regular. Codetta II of the exposition reappears as Section II of the coda.

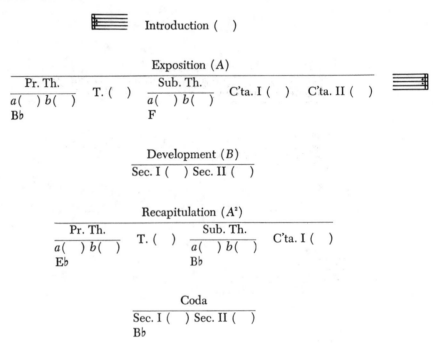

Attention is called to the joint repeat of the introduction and exposition. Graphs only are given in our next three examples.

Example 114.   Beethoven, Symphony No. 7, First Movement

$$\frac{\text{Introduction}}{a(10+4+8) \to b(11) \to a(8) \to b^2(11) \to}$$
$$\quad\; A \qquad\qquad C \qquad \text{Mod.} \quad F$$

T. (10)

---

[12] See also Mozart's Piano Sonata, K. 545.

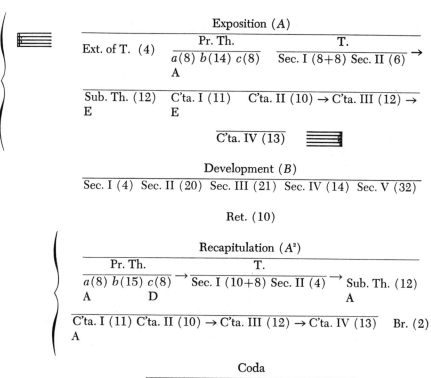

Example 115. Brahms, Symphony No. 3, First Movement

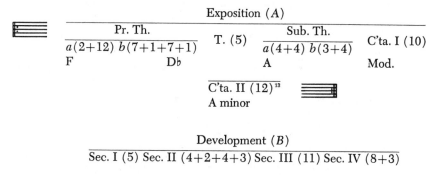

[13] 11 measures by second ending.

Example 116.   Franck, Symphony in D Minor, First Movement

Exposition (*A*)

Pr. Th.				Pr. Th.[14]		
a				*a*		
a(12) *b*(4) *a*²(12)		*b*(10+10)		*a*(12) *b*(4) *a*²(12)		*b*(10+8)
D minor				F minor		

	T. (4)	Sub. Th.		C'ta. I (26)	C'ta. II (8)
		a(12+18) *b*(16)			
		F D♭ F			

Development (*B*)

Sec. I (20) Sec. II (14) Sec. III (14) Sec. IV (18) Sec. V (22)

Sec. VI (29)   Ret. (35)

Recapitulation (*A*²)

Pr. Th.		T. (4)	Sub. Th.		C'ta. I (26)
a(14+4) *b*(12+24)			*a*(12+18) *b*(16)		
D minor E♭ minor			D D		

C'ta. II (12)

Coda

Sec. I (20) Sec. II (20) Sec. III (9)

The music of Sibelius is unique and extremely personal both in musical content and the use of form. This is evident in all seven of his symphonies. He used sonata-form but never more than it served his purposes as a creator of music. The first movement of his Fourth Symphony has been selected for analysis because it shows how he dealt with the form in one important instance and gives an insight as well into his mastery of motives, the hallmark of the true symphonist. The tight merging of the parts at times renders it difficult, if not impossible, to fix a precise division point. There are no block cadences; even the final cadence is defined melodically.

The two motives which prove such potent formative forces are introduced within the first seven measures: Motive *A* is heard at the very beginning and Motive *B* at the seventh measure. The basso ostinato, which continues, with slight interruption, throughout the primary theme, is set off by Motive *A* and, indeed, may be interpreted as an extension of it. The primary and subordinate themes are both based on Motive *B*. Motive *A* reappears in the coda. Section I of the development is about equally dependent on both motives. The music here is thinned down to a single line and for a time takes on the spirit of a recitative.

Section II is an astonishing feat of motivic manipulation. The extent to which Motive *A* dominates this section of the development cannot be appreciated by a mere glance at the open score. The muted violins and violas (later joined by the cellos) pursue three closely associated melodic lines. The motive, used continuously, is spun through the whole fabric of the section. The figuration

[14] Pr. Th. repeated in sequence.

In our reduction, this structure is made clear by the heavy notes. Against the subdued and evanescent background of the massed upper strings are heard greatly augmented versions of the same motive in the woodwinds, low strings, and occasionally the horns. In measure 80 the clarinet announces an independent motive which is repeated later by the flute, the oboe, and the clarinet itself.

The primary theme is omitted in the recapitulation. We have already mentioned that such omissions are common in Sibelius' music.

Scales other than the usual major and minor may be observed in this movement. A lydian atmosphere is produced at the first sounding of Motive A and becomes rather general in the second section of the development. (The lydian scale is equivalent to the major scale with a raised fourth degree.) The coda is written on the scale

which is sometimes called the Neapolitan major.

The student should have recourse to a full score and, by all means, listen to a good recording. Most of the reduction can be performed on a piano, but the first purpose in offering it was to bring the composition into sharper focus. The rapid string passages in the development cannot be satisfactorily reproduced on a keyboard.

Example 117.   Sibelius, Symphony No. 4, First Movement[15] (Reduction by Paul Fontaine)

Introduction

Molto moderato, quasi adagio

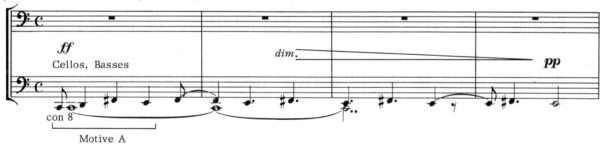

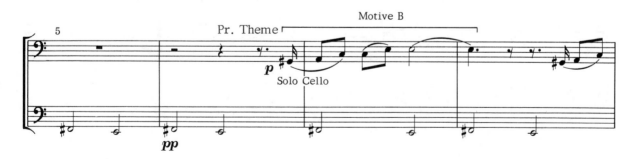

Digression to G-flat.

This digression to C with a raised fourth is in the lydian mode.

Episode

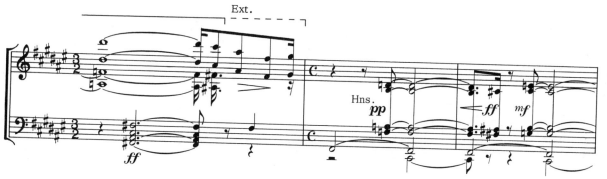

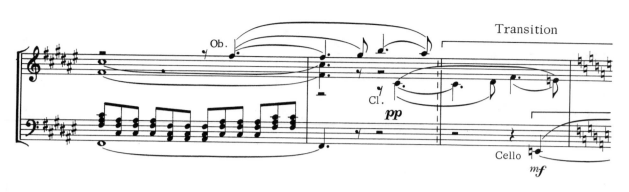

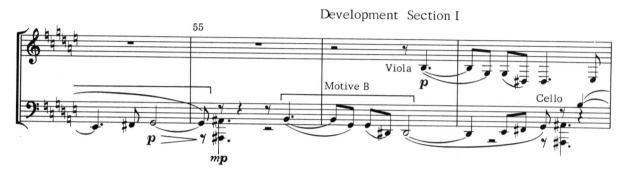

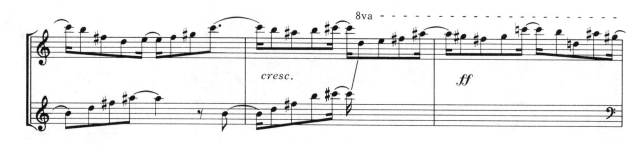

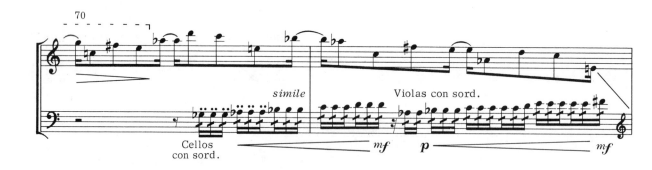

Section II   Greatly augmented version of Motive A

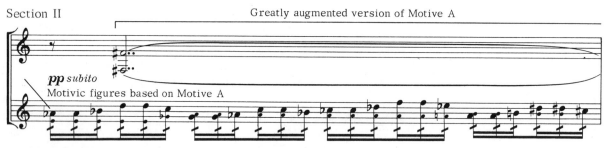

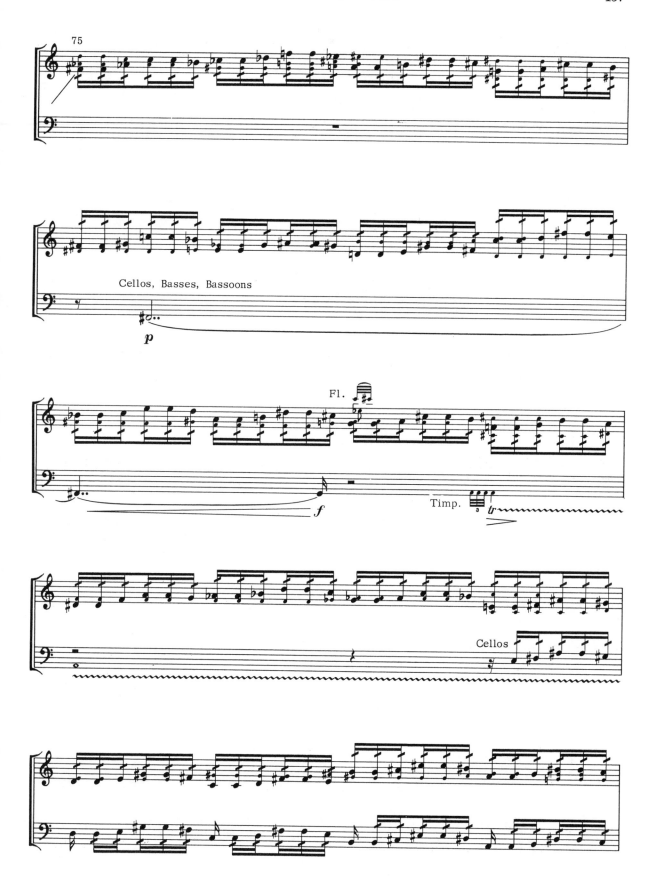

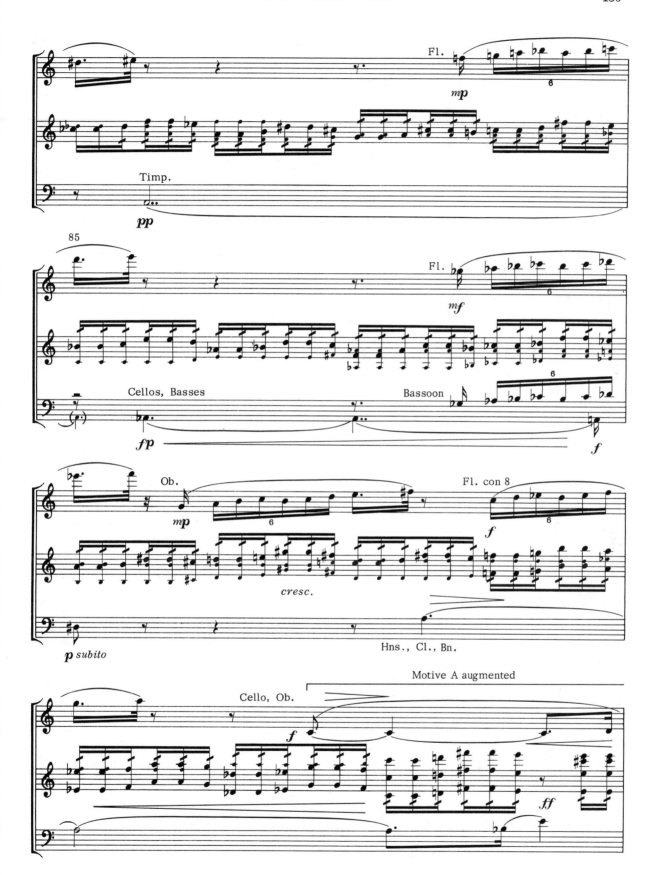

Sibelius, Symphony No. 4, First Movement

Exposition (A)

Intro. (6)   Pr. Th. (22) → Ep. (11) Br. (1)   Sub. Th.

A minor   a(7) b(5)

F#

Development (B)

T (3)   Sec. I (16)   Sec. II (16) →

Recapitulation (A²)   → Coda (5)

Ep. (8) Br. (1)   Sub. Th.   A

a(7) b(6)

A

In closing this series of studies in sonata-form it can be seen that a great reliance has been placed on graphs. While a graph can afford no idea at all of the musical qualities of a piece of music, it does have a direct utility in the special field of *form*. No student can make a correct graph without careful and detailed study of the score. If he does this he will be likely to remember the material before him.

If the graphs in this chapter have been used in confirming analyses of the compositions involved, the making of graphs of other compositions should not be too difficult.

SUGGESTED ASSIGNMENTS

1. Make graphs of first movements of the following:
   Sonata, Opus 2, No. 1, Beethoven
   Sonata, Opus 10, No. 1, Beethoven
   Sonata, Opus 13, Beethoven
   Sonata, Opus 31, No. 3, Beethoven
   Any of Haydn's symphonies
   Symphony in E-flat, Mozart
   Symphony No. 3, Beethoven
   Symphony No. 5, Beethoven
   Symphony No. 1, Brahms
   A string quartet selected from the works of Haydn or Mozart or the early works of Beethoven.
2. Include with each graph a written outline, emphasizing and clarifying your analysis with short quotations from the music, as was done in this chapter with Examples 107, 108, and 109.
3. Give special attention to all development sections. This means that every measure of music should be explained (at least in context). Is it new material? Is it derivative? If the latter, explain, giving sources.

---

[16] Note that the subordinate theme is first heard in the major submediant.

9

Forms Related to the Sonata

If these studies followed their chronological order the so-called abbreviated, or binary, sonata-form would be taken up prior to the classical sonata. However, there is something to be said for deferring the subject until after a full study of sonata-form when other related forms can be taken up at the same time. The latter course is followed in this book in the belief that the student will better appreciate deviations, modifications, or unusual adaptations of the form.

BINARY SONATA-FORM

At the beginning of Chapter 8 we saw that formerly almost any instrumental piece might be called a sonata. It is not surprising that countless small two-part compositions were included. The typical binary sonata-form comprises a primary and a subordinate theme with possibly a closing theme or codetta. Its distinguishing feature is the total lack of a development. The tonic-dominant or tonic-relative major key relationship is usually present in the first part (exposition), but the return to the tonic key at the recapitulation did not at once become standard practice. Baroque and early classical composers preferred not to change keys in crossing the double bar: this is illustrated in Example 118 taken from a short piece by Domenico Scarlatti (1685–1757) which is clearly in binary sonata-form.

Example 118. Scarlatti, D., Sonata (Longo 463, Kirk. 430)

Exposition (A)

Primary Theme (19)

Subordinate Theme (22)

Closing Theme (Codetta) (13)

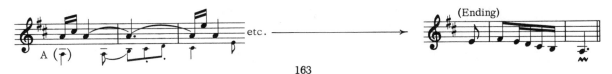

Recapitulation (B or A²)

Primary Theme (19)

Subordinate Theme (22)

Closing Theme (Codetta) (13)

Notice that the primary theme (Example 119) returns in the key of the relative major, the key of the preceding subordinate theme. This means a change of mode from its first sounding.

Example 119.   Haydn, Sonata No. 17, Second Movement (Andante)

Exposition (A)		
Pr. Th. (14)	Sub. Th. (10)	
G minor F	Bb	

Recapitulation (B or A²)		
Pr. Th. (18)	Sub. Th. (10)	
Bb	D G minor	

Beethoven uses a single chord, the dominant seventh, to re-establish the tonic A-flat, at the recapitulation (Example 120).

Example 120.   Beethoven, Sonata, Opus 10, No. 1, Second Movement (Adagio Molto)

Exposition (A)			
Pr. Th. (16)	T. (7)	Sub. Th. (12+9)	Br. (1)
Ab		Eb	(V⁷)

Recapitulation (B or A²)		
Pr. Th. (16)	T. (9)	Sub. Th. (12+8)
Ab	. . . .	
	Coda (22)	
	. . . .	

THE SONATINA

Pieces called sonatinas appeared as early as the mid-seventeenth century. There is, quite naturally, the same confusion as to form that we observed in the evolution of the sonata. It will save time and facilitate our task to dismiss the hundreds of small two- and three-part pieces (many of them in the elementary class) which are still preserved in collections of so-called sonatinas and concentrate on more modern examples which have some honest claim to the title.

The word *sonatina* is a diminutive form of *sonata*, just as we have other words like *rondino*, *scherzino*, *fughetta*, *canzonetta*, and the like. This means that, if properly used, it should be confined to pieces which, while small in their dimensions, possess at least a semblance of the essential construction of full sonata-form. We may be guided by the practices of composers of the recent past and even of our own time, for the sonatina is still a popular form.

A development section as understood in the sonata is foreign to the sonatina. Ravel's *sonatine* (Example 122) is somewhat exceptional but even here the tendency is to repeat themes rather than develop them. Usually there is a brief new theme or, more often, a few simple measures of transitional character.

The distinctive characteristics of a sonatina may be summarized as (1) brevity of parts, (2) no development but, in its stead, a short independent theme or transitional passage, and (3) music of a light and uncomplicated nature. The great majority were written for instructional purposes, mostly for the piano. As such, they are the only compositions that keep the names of certain composers from total oblivion—every student of piano will easily recall Clementi, Kuhlau, and Dussek. However, Beethoven and Mozart left several excellent sonatinas. Actually, many of the early sonatas of Mozart and Haydn are really sonatinas, while a few modern sonatinas, by the same criterion, approximate full-length sonatas.

Only two graphs, selected from recently composed sonatinas, will be given. These can be supplemented, if desired, by additional examples from easily available sources.

Example 121. Kabalevsky, Sonatina, Opus 13, No. 1, First Movement

Exposition (*A*)
_____
Pr. Th.
$\overline{a(8)\ b(18)}$ T. (5)   Sub. Th. (20) C'ta. (12)
C   G .   .   .   .   .   .

Middle Theme (*B*)
$\overline{a(12)\ b(16)}$ T. (4)

Recapitulation (*A²*)
_____
Pr. Th.
$\overline{a(8)\ b(15)}$ Sub. Th. (16)   C'ta. (4)
C .   .   .   .

Coda (4)
.   .   .   .

Example 122. Ravel, Sonatine, First Movement

Exposition (*A*)
_____
Pr. Th. (12) → Sub. Th. (7) C'ta. (4+2)   T. (5½)
F♯ minor   C♯ minor

Middle Theme (*B*)
$\overline{a(8½)\ b(12+4)} →$

Recapitulation (A²)

Pr. Th. (12) → Sub. Th. (7) C'ta. (4+2)
F♯ minor   F♯ . . .

Coda (4)

. . .

The overbearing weight of first movements, as opposed to later movements, is quite obvious in many of Beethoven's early sonatas as well as the sonatas and symphonies of Haydn and Mozart. The music of strongest impact was almost always delivered in the first movement (usually in sonata-form) while the final movement was in lighter vein, an allegro or a rondo in which gaiety and brilliance were stressed rather than depth. Beethoven rebelled against this practice with increasing vehemence— witness the great Rondo of Sonata, Opus 53, the long and involved fugue of the *Hammerklavier Sonata*, Opus 106, or, as a crowning example, the chorale finale of the Ninth Symphony.

In his Sonatas Opus 101 and 109, Beethoven used a different approach. Here he deliberately played down the importance of the first movement, mainly by the simple expedient of brevity. Let us focus attention on the first movement of Opus 101, which is compressed to a hundred and two measures requiring but three minutes of playing time. It has occasionally been classed as a sonatina, an understandable conclusion if one looks no further than its proportions. But examining it more closely, we hear a melodic line that flows easily, with so little change of rhythm and no sharp cadences that the parts do not stand out with the usual contrast. The primary theme is abbreviated in the recapitulation. Short as the movement is, the development (with the transition in which development continues) is longer proportionately than in several other examples that have come before us. The fact that there is a development removes this miniature from the general classification of sonatina in a technical sense. But the severe brevity represents a modification of sonata-form—certainly so in the world of Beethoven.

Example 123.   Beethoven, Sonata, Opus 101, First Movement

Exposition (A)

Pr. Th. (16) → Sub. Th. (9) C'ta. (9) →
A   E

$$\frac{\text{Development } (B)}{\text{One section (18)}} \to \text{T. (5)} \to$$

Recapitulation (A²)

Pr. Th. (11) → Sub. Th. (9) C'ta. (10) →   Coda (15)
A . . . .

There is a certain modification of sonata-form in which a development, possibly in several sections, takes place *after* the recapitulation is underway. Study the graph in Example 124. The primary theme returns immediately after the codetta of the exposition as we saw in the abbreviated, or binary, sonata-form. Then follows the unexpected—a full-scale development is interposed before the return of the subordinate theme. Such a design has been categorized by some analysts as "enlarged sonatina-form," or simply "sonatina-allegro form."

Such designations seem grossly unrealistic, even though they have a limited acceptance. A bona-fide development, often of major proportions, is there, and this is not a feature native to the sonatina. Because of this fact and the length of most of these movements the form is more comparable to the sonata than to the sonatina, the only point of difference being the delayed development. The word "sonatina" has an historic connotation of smallness of size, as do all other diminutive titles in music, that should be respected. There is at least equal reason to label the form "enlarged binary sonata-form." It is, in effect, sonata-form with a *delayed development* but any special designation conveying this information is likely to be too cumbersome for popular usage.

Example 124. Brahms, Symphony No. 3, Fourth Movement

Exposition (A)

Pr. Th.	
$\overline{a(18)\ b(11)\ c(6)}$	T. (16)
F minor D F minor	

Sub. Th.

$\overline{a(10)\ b(13)}$

C

Codetta

$\overline{\text{Sec. I (16) Sec. II (5) Sec. III (8)}}$

Ret. (4)

Recapitulation (A²)

Pr. Th.

$\overline{a(12+14)}$

F minor

Development

$\overline{\text{Sec. I (15) Sec. II (23) Sec. III (7)}}$

T. (15)	Sub. Th.
	$\overline{a(10)\ b(13)}$
	F .

Codetta

$\overline{\text{Sec. I (16) Sec. II (5) Sec. III (9)}}$

	Coda
T. (6)	$\overline{\text{Sec. I (9) Sec. II (5) Sec. III (14) Sec. IV (16) Sec. V (13)}}$

See also Beethoven's Quartet, Opus 95 (finale), the Finale of Brahms's Symphony in C minor, and the *Tragic Overture*.

THE SONATA-RONDO

The reason for deferring attention to the sonata-rondo until after a thorough study of sonata-form itself will be immediately evident. The two forms resemble each other in that there is a primary and a subordinate theme with the same key relationships usually observed. The sonata-rondo may also be regarded as a ternary design, but to a lesser degree. As the name suggests, it is a blending of the rondo and sonata-form.

The dissimilarities are important. In the sonata-rondo are to be noted:

1. The recurrence, *after* the subordinate theme, of the primary theme in both the exposition and the recapitulation. Thus in a sonata-rondo the primary theme is heard at least four times.

2. The general lack of development in the middle theme or episode.[1]

3. The more tune-like quality of the primary theme in most sonata-rondos. This invites a lightness and even gaiety not usually found in the primary theme of a sonata. However, since extensive fragmentation and motivic development are not common in the middle theme of a rondo, they are not heavily considered in selecting a primary theme.

---

[1] In the sonata-rondo we are confining the word "episode" to the middle theme, which occurs but once.

Compare the following outline of sonata-rondo form with that of sonata-form.

	Introduction (optional)	
Exposition	Primary Theme	*Tonic*
	Subordinate Theme	*Usually dominant or relative major*
	(Transition)	
	Primary Theme	*Tonic*
Episode	Usually new and unrestricted as to key.	
	Rarely shows developmental techniques.	
	(Transition)	
Recapitulation	Primary Theme	*Tonic*
	Subordinate Theme	*Tonic*
	(Transition)	
	Primary Theme	*Tonic*
	Coda	Coda may displace primary theme if based on same material.

Beethoven did more than any other composer to establish the sonata-rondo as a major form. Our first example is taken from one of his best-known works.

Example 125. Beethoven, Sonata, Opus 13, Third Movement

Exposition

Primary Theme, C Minor

Transition (18–24)

Subordinate Theme, E-Flat Major

Codetta, E-Flat Major (44–50)

Transition (51–62). Modulates back to C minor. Built on a motive from Part II of the subordinate theme.

Primary Theme (63–79). As at first.

Episode, A-Flat Major

Part I (80-99)

Part II (100-107)

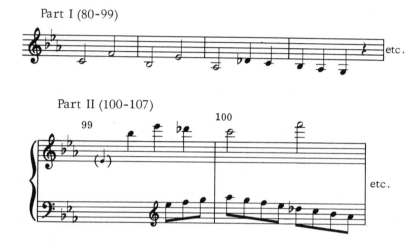

Transition (108–121). Modulates back to C minor.

Primary Theme. Part I (122–129) is as found at first.

Part II (130–134) is much shortened and is fused directly, without cadence, to the subordinate theme which appears now in the tonic major. Measures 132 and 133 are a modification in the form of a sequence. They provide, with measure 134, a bridge in place of the original transition which is omitted.

The codetta (159 et seq.) is extended as a transition. The primary theme is heard in measures 172–182. Only Part I is heard here. The coda (183–211) can be broken down into three codettas or sections: 183–193; 194–203; and 204–211.

Beethoven, Rondo, Sonata, Opus 13

	Exposition				
Primary Th.	T. (7) →	Sub. Th.	T. (11) →	Primary Th.	
$\overline{a(8)\ b(9)}$		$\overline{a(8)\ b(11)\ \text{C'ta. (8)}}$		$\overline{a(8)\ b(9)}$	
C minor		E♭		C minor	

	Episode	
	$\overline{\text{Sec. I (8+12) Sec. II (8)}}$	T. (14) →
	A♭	

	Recapitulation			
Primary Th.	→	Sub. Th.	T. (13) →	Primary Th.
$\overline{a(8)\ b(5)}$		$\overline{a(9)\ b(11)\ \text{C'ta. (4)}}$ →		$\overline{a(8+4)}$
C minor		C		C minor

	Coda	
	$\overline{\text{Sec. I (4+ 7) Sec. II (9)} \rightarrow \text{Sec. III (8)}}$	
	C minor	

Saint-Saëns' *Introduction and Rondo Capriccioso* for violin and orchestra, one of the world's most popular violin virtuoso pieces for over three quarters of a century, offers a superlative example of the sonata-rondo form in its most perfected state. The composer has omitted nothing that could in good taste have been included.

It should be noted that the second section of the first transition in the recapitulation is an important, independent, and fully cadenced melody heard only at this spot. It is therefore an episode and is so indicated. The numbers in brackets *before* a part indicate measures in which an accompanimental pattern is started before the entrance of the theme.

Example 126. Saint-Saëns, Introduction and Rondo Capriccioso, Opus 28

	Introduction	
	$\overline{\text{(2) Sec. I (16) Sec. II (14)}}$	Br. (4)
	A minor	

		Exposition			
(4)	Pr. Th.	Sub. Th. (15)	T. (18)	Pr. Th. (22)	
	$\overline{a(16)\ b(16)}$				
	A minor C	C		A minor	

	Middle Theme (Episode)	
T. (23)	$\overline{\text{(2) } a(16) \qquad b(14)}$	T. (17)
	C E	

	Recapitulation		
	T.		
Pr. Th. (22)	$\overline{\text{Sec. I (13) Sec. II (Ep.) (21)}}$	Sub. Th. (15)	T. (16)
A minor	A minor F F		

$\overline{\text{Pr. Th. (17)}}$	Cadenza (1)	Br. (4)	Coda (34)
A minor			A

THE CLASSICAL CONCERTO

The classical solo concerto is brought to attention here only because of the *double exposition*, which was common practice until well into the nineteenth century. The exploitation of instrumental contrast, inherited from the old concerto grosso, significantly influenced form. Usually, the double exposition worked out as follows: all important themes were first heard in the orchestra, then repeated by the soloist, each in regular sonata order. The orchestral exposition was generally in the tonic key throughout, leaving to the soloist the subordinate excursion into closely related keys.

An excellent example may be seen in Mozart's justly popular Concerto for Piano and Orchestra in A, K. 488. The first phrases of the primary and subordinate themes are:

Example 127.

Primary Theme

Subordinate Theme

Double Exposition

	Orchestra		
Pr. Th. (17)	T. (13)	Sub. Th.	
		a(16) *b*(16) C'ta. (4)	
A		A	

	Piano		
Pr. Th. (15)	Tutti (5)	T (12)	Sub. Th.
A			*a*(15) *b*(23)
			E

A double exposition is an actuality in Example 127. Both orchestra and soloist present in turn all important thematic material used in a movement. This is not always the case even in the classical solo concertos. One finds that the solo instrument may at times enter with a new theme, or that the orchestra may have announced some of the themes but not all of them. Such expositions are not really double, but rather *shared* expositions, or one complete exposition divided into two parts. But they have been so persistently regarded by teachers as double expositions that it seems advisable to accept this terminology, if the reservations are understood.

The next two examples will clarify the point. Both are taken from Mozart, the most important writer of concertos before Beethoven.

In the Concerto in D minor (Example 128) the closing theme (orchestra) is not given to the piano at any time. It is heard again at the end of the movement in the orchestra. Part *b* of the primary theme (orchestra) becomes, in effect, a transition later in the piano, modulating to C, dominant of F, the relative major. The subordinate theme is reserved for the piano.

The new theme at the entrance of the solo part is not found in the recapitulation but is used in the development. Functionally, it stands as a sort of introduction to the return of the primary theme in the second exposition.

The long transition in the primary theme (orchestra) is missing in the second exposition.

The student should note that in totalling measures for parts, sections, or codettas, if a new part begins *simultaneously* with a cadence chord (i.e., a chord of resolution), that whole measure is assigned to the new part. If the new section begins as an upbeat (i.e., as a partial measure *after* a cadence chord), that whole measure is assigned to the preceding part.

Example 128.   Mozart, Exposition, Concerto in D Minor, K. 466

	Orchestra			
Pr. Th.	Sub. Th. (12)	T (5)	Cl. Th. (12+10)	C'ta. (6)
a(16) *b*(16) F	D minor		D minor	
D minor				

	Piano		
New Th. (13) Tutti (4)	Pr. Th. *a*(17) Tutti (3)		Sub. Th.
D minor	D minor		*a*(13) *b*(8) tutti (8)
			F

Coda		
Sec. I (9) Sec. II (6) Sec. III (16)		
F		

Example 129 is much nearer to a double exposition than the previous example. However, there are important differences between the two expositions. The transitional material (piano) is not the same as that in the orchestra. The closing theme (orchestra) is not heard in the piano. The subordinate theme in the piano is expanded in a flashy, eighteenth-century manner.

Example 129.   Mozart, Exposition, Concerto in A, K. 414

	Orchestra			
Pr. Th. (16)	T. (16)	Sub. Th. (18)	Cl. Th. (7)	C'ta. (6)
A		A	A	

	Piano			
Pr. Th. (16)	C'ta. (6)	T. (20+9)	Sub. Th. (22)	C'ta. (8+8)
A			E	E

The solo concerto as a form must be compared to the symphony in dimension, although it is almost always in three movements. The display of virtuosity, ever a conscious goal, led to the expansion of transitions, frequent interpolations of technical flights, the inevitable cadenza, and often (especially in the modern concerto) a coda of impressive length.

In time the orchestral exposition went out of fashion, but it died gradually. In his first three piano concertos Beethoven began with an orchestral exposition but in his fourth and fifth he broke away to entrust an introduction to the solo instrument. This portended things to come, even though Beethoven still held to the double exposition. However, after the examples set by Mendelssohn and

SUGGESTED ASSIGNMENTS

1. Investigate the Adagio of Mozart's Sonata, K. 332 as an example of binary sonata form.
2. The binary sonata-form has been much used in overtures. Study Beethoven's *Prometheus* Overture, Mozart's Overture to *The Marriage of Figaro*, or Schubert's Overture to *Rosamunde*. Such compositions as these prove that the "abbreviated" or binary sonata may actually be of large dimensions, contrary to a sonatina.
3. Select one of Clementi's sonatinas (not the first one in C) and compare it to Ravel's Sonatina. Confine your observations to the first movements and to *form* only. A representative sonatina by Kuhlau or Dussek will serve as well.
4. Make a comparison between the Dussek or Clementi sonatina and any of Haydn's first eighteen sonatas and be prepared to present in class a definite opinion, based on first-hand information, concerning the status of Haydn's early sonatas as examples of sonata-form.
5. Study Beethoven's two sonatas, Opus 49, Nos. 1 and 2. Are they really sonatinas? Why or why not?
6. See final movements of Beethoven's Sonatas Opus 2, No. 2; Opus 2, No. 3; Opus 7; Opus 10, No. 3; Opus 22; Opus 28; Opus 31, No. 3; and Opus 53. (Be especially alert in the last of these suggested rondos. There is a long coda.) Make a graph of at least one of the above.
7. Examine Mendelssohn's *Rondo Capriccioso* for piano. This is excellent concert music but it is not accepted as a model sonata-rondo. Explain why. Can it be explained as a rondo at all?
8. Make a similar study of Mendelssohn's Scherzo from the *Midsummer Night's Dream*.
9. Analyze fully and make a graph of the expositions of the first movement of Beethoven's Concerto in C minor.
10. Analyze and compare the expositions of:
    Concerto for Piano in A minor, Schumann
    Concerto for Violin in D, Beethoven
    Any of the piano concertos of Mozart not brought up in this chapter.
    Concerto for Violin in E minor, Mendelssohn

    (Note: The Schumann and Mendelssohn concertos do not have double expositions. They are suggested for comparison only.)

10

The Canon

We have already had occasion to refer to certain short canons and to define them as pieces in which a melody is heard in counterpoint against itself (p. 95). They could also be defined as polyphonic pieces in two or more voices in which the element of imitation is absolute.

In Renaissance and Baroque times the canon was developed to such perfection that the great surviving masterpieces stand as unsurpassable examples of what can be achieved in the art of strict imitation. While more recent composers have not been so intrigued by complicated canonical constructions as were the old masters, the canon as a serious and useful musical device has never been obsolete. A number of nineteenth century romanticists were attracted to it, among them Schubert, Mendelssohn, Schumann, and Grieg, and composers of our own day have turned to it often.

Canons appear in a wide variety of forms and types. Some of these have a proven practical value while others are sheer oddities bearing about the same relation to music that a jigsaw puzzle does to art. We will be guided by this observation in making our selection of examples.

The construction of a canon starts with the fixing of two all-important intervals—the *pitch* interval, which determines the vertical relationship of the voices and the *time* interval, which marks the linear distance between the melody in the leading voice and the imitation of the melody in the following voice.

By far the most frequent pitch interval is the octave, either above or below the first voice. Only this interval permits the *exact* imitation of all melodic movement without threatening the tonality. This can be illustrated very simply. Suppose our first voice begins:

This figure dips a minor second below *c*, the tonic tone, returns to ascend a major third, a minor third, finally turning back a major second. Transpose this to the successive steps of the C major scale.

Chromatic alterations are required in each instance to preserve the exact intervals of the original figure. Literal imitations at intervals other than the octave would thus produce the effect of two keys sounding simultaneously. In practice such alterations are not used. This means, to return to our illustration, that an imitation at *any* interval generally is held to the scale of the tonic; thus:

174

and so on, regardless of the fact that major intervals may be answered by minor ones or vice versa.

The time interval in canons varies greatly. In many canons it is a single beat (see Variation 6 of the Brahms Variations, Chapter 7). It may be a half-measure, a full measure, or more. It is preferable that it not be too long an interval, as the effectiveness of a canon, as such, depends on the quick reiteration in the following voice of every detail, especially accents, of the leading voice. In other words, the *diagonal* relationship between voices, which is the distinctive feature of a canon, should be clear throughout.

CANONS AT THE OCTAVE

In Example 130 the pitch interval is the lower octave, the time interval a half-measure. This and the two following canons are fully harmonized.

Example 130. Schumann, *Symphonic Studies*, Opus 13

Example 131.   Grieg, Canon, Opus 38, No. 8

Example 132.   Franck, Sonata in A Major for Piano and Violin

CANONS AT THE UNISON

Canons at the *unison* are similar to those at the octave in that the imitation does not shift the melody up or down scale. The difference is one of register. At the unison the voices are closely interwoven and a great deal of crossing is inevitable. See Bach's *Goldberg Variations* (No. 3) for what is perhaps the world's most famous example of a canon *all' unisono*.

CANONS AT THE FIFTH

After the octave, the fifth is the most used pitch interval. Good examples of canons *alla quinta* may be found in the choral works of Palestrina and Bach. Example 133 includes the first phrase of a chorale accompanied by a canon at the fifth. There is a modulation to the dominant and a return to the tonic. Study the small changes in the imitation caused by the *f-sharp*.

Example 133.   Bach, Variation on Chorale *Vom Himmel hoch*

etc.

In Example 134 the lowest voice (tenor) is in canon at the lower fifth with the alto, while the alto is in canon, also at the fifth, with the soprano. This automatically places the tenor in canon at the ninth with the soprano, a relationship that also had to be reckoned with.

Example 134. Palestrina, Mass *Ad Fugam*

CANONS IN AUGMENTATION

This is a comparatively rare type. Its disadvantage is that the time interval between points of imitation constantly grows until the canon can no longer be heard as such by anyone who has not analyzed it in advance.

Example 135.   Bach, *Variations on a Christmas Song* (Extra voices omitted)

Example 136.   Arensky, Suite in Canon-Form, Opus 65[1]

Notice that in six measures the time interval increases from zero to three full measures.

[1] By permission of the copyright owner, G. Schirmer, Inc., New York.

DOUBLE CANONS, OR CANONS WITH TWO THEMES

A double canon is of necessity in four parts or voices. The difficulty of writing one is understandably much greater than that attending a simple canon. Example 137 is an excerpt from an organ prelude in which a chorale is itself heard in canon while an accompanying canon in shorter notes is given to the manuals. The complete work may be found in the Bach-Gesellschaft Edition. A reference to this will show that the composer's task was not always so easy as it appears here.

Example 137.   Bach, Organ Prelude *In dulci jubilo* (Voices in free counterpoint omitted)

CANONS BY CONTRARY MOTION

This is also known as the mirroring technique. Every melodic movement of the leading voice is answered by a similar movement in the opposite direction in the following voice. This procedure is continued throughout Example 138.

There are other points of interest, too, here. The pitch interval is changed several times. Beginning at the sixth, sections follow at the third, second, and finally the ninth. In canons such as this, involving melodic inversion, the pitch interval is reckoned from the *first* note in the imitation (see diagonal lines).

Example 138.   Bach, *Variations on a Christmas Song* (Voices in free counterpoint omitted)

In the next example both canons are by contrary motion.

Example 139.   Mozart, Serenade in C Minor

Example 140 is quoted from a piece written for piano solo. When the piece is played, the effect is that of a series of sonorities liberally spiced with dissonance. There are, however, four melodic lines forming a double canon at the octave.

Example 140.   Persichetti, Sonatine No. 2[2]

[2] Permission for reprint granted by Elkan-Vogel Co., Inc., Philadelphia, copyright owners.

Our final example is a double canon quoted from a symphony by Anton Webern. Both canons are by contrary motion, the second voice being an inversion of the first in each case. The instrumentation is carefully indicated since the matter of timbres was a most important consideration with this composer. Those who are interested in modern trends in music should note that both canons are based on the same twelve-tone row.

The row is symmetrical in that the interval arrangement is the same read from either end. No tone is repeated in the row but may be repeated in the canon, provided its position in the row is not disturbed. Some of the intervals are spelled enharmonically; for example, in the lower canon the minor third *f–a*-flat (measures 2 and 3) is answered in the transposed inversion by the augmented second *c*-sharp–*b*-flat. In measure 7, tones 6 and 7 (reading up) are sounded simultaneously in the lower canon and answered in the same manner. Many of the intervals are expanded by one or two octaves and may be inverted at the same time. The major sixth (measures 1 and 2) is an inversion of the minor third seen in the row. The *g* (measure 3, same voice) is displaced downward two octaves and forms a minor ninth, instead of a minor second, with the following *a*-flat (*a*-flat = *g*-sharp). Pursue similar points throughout the example, but remember that the row in Canon II has been transposed to begin on *f*.

Example 141.   Webern, Symphony for Small Orchestra, Opus 21[3]

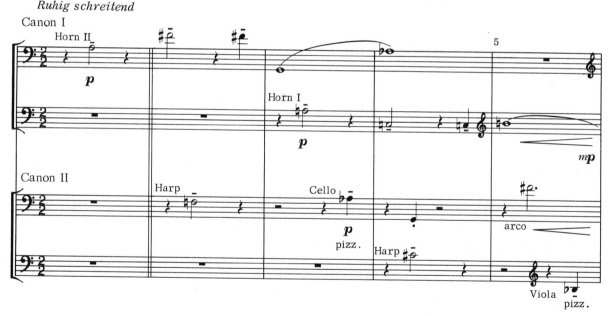

[3] Copyright 1929 by Universal Edition, renewed 1956 by Anton Webern's heirs. Reprinted by permission of Theodore Presser Co., Bryn Mawr, Pa., agents.

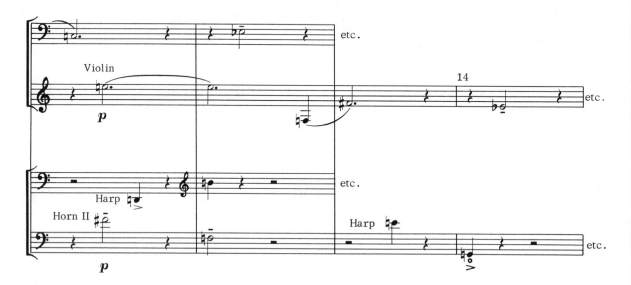

THE ROUND

There is a type of canon known as the round. It is also called a circle, or perpetual, canon. There are a number of popular examples in folk music. Academically, such creations are sometimes referred as *infinite* canons, because they are constructed in such a way that they may run on infinitely. Although J. S. Bach wrote many of them (see *The Musical Offering*) and probably improvised many more, they must have been considered by him, and by the numerous other composers who indulged in them, as a pastime or amusement more than as serious art, notwithstanding the cleverness required to put them together. Since the word "infinite" has been used to describe these canons, it follows that all canons which end in a terminating cadence are *finite*.

Certain fundamental conclusions about the canon may be summed up as follows:

1. Any pitch interval (except augmented or diminished intervals) may be used, although the octave is the most common.
2. Any time interval may be used, but a short one is favored. In 4/4 or *alla breve* meters a half- or full measure is most common. In shorter meters a full measure or more is most common.

3. Imitation by augmentation is the least practical arrangement because of the ever-expanding time interval.
4. A canon is *accompanied* if free parts are added.
5. There is no fixed rule limiting the number of voices, but the great majority of canons are of the simple type (i.e., two voices).
6. A double canon is a combination of two simple canons.

Those who wish to pursue the study of the canon into some of the more unusual forms are referred to Bach's *The Musical Offering*. Examples of triple or even quadruple canon may be found in works of Mozart. See his Mass in D, No. 7 and the *Requiem*.

We have been dealing exclusively with *complete* canons; that is, pieces or sections of pieces which follow a chosen canonical pattern to a cadence. Attention should be called to the probable truth that isolated passages in canon, heard as details in large compositions, represent a more important use of the technique of strict imitation. A few illustrations, picked at random, will illustrate the point.

Mendelssohn, *Variations Sérieuses*, Var. 4

Brahms, Intermezzo, Opus 117, No. 1

Hindemith, Piano Sonata No. 2[4], First Movement

[4] Copyright 1936, renewed 1963 by B. Schott's Soehne/Mainz. Reprinted by permission.

SUGGESTED ASSIGNMENTS

1. Examine the *Goldberg Variations* of J. S. Bach and make a written report answering the following questions:
   Which variations are in canon form?
   What are the pitch and time intervals of each?
   Which canons are accompanied?
   Are there canons by augmentation? Contrary motion?
2. Make as full a report as you can on canons from the standard literature not mentioned in this text.
3. Seek out and report on short passages in strict imitation similar to those on page 185.
4. For the student who is interested in composition, arranging, or the teaching of any branch of music, the creation of short original canons at various time and pitch intervals is valuable experience. In no other way can the peculiar problems of the canon be better appreciated. The playing of original canons in class can be great fun.

11

The Fugue

There is such a diversity of pieces existing under the name of *fugue* that even defining the word is well-nigh impossible. To speak of a "fugal form," as though there were some master mold into which all fugues should fit, is to imply an untruth. One can generalize that most fugues show a ternary basic structure; others do not, however, and the difference seems to have nothing to do with their being accepted as fugues.

A large number of small fugues reveal a shadowy resemblance to the simple rondo in that there is an exposition, a middle section, and a sort of recapitulation, all based on the same subject, with connecting episodes. But the resemblance should not be taken too seriously—fugue writers are not likely to have the rondo in mind.

A polyphonic texture may be taken for granted, but extended homophonic passages are to be found in many fugues. The greatest master of fugue, J. S. Bach, exercised considerable freedom in the mechanics of instrumental polyphony. In the forty-eight fugues which make up *The Well-Tempered Clavier,* he begins each with a selected number of voices (usually three or four) and, with few exceptional passages, accounts for that number of voices throughout.[1] In his *Art of Fugue,* written surely with an educational aim in mind, he is quite particular about this matter. But in certain other fugues, such as the familiar Toccata and Fugue in D minor for organ, he makes little pretense after the exposition of adhering to a definite number of voices. One might investigate the same point with Mendelssohn's *Six Fugues,* Opus 35, for piano, or Brahms's fugue from the *Variations on a Theme by Handel.*

It is only in the exposition that we find, in spite of the great variety of styles and procedures, all fugues conforming to certain common rules. We will treat this opening section with special care. Later we will examine several fugues in their entirety, hoping to prepare the student to make further analyses on his own.

As a first important step, the following definitions should be studied and memorized.

Subject: a word preferred to "theme" in dealing with the fugue. This consists of a short melodic idea, usually a phrase, first heard at the beginning of the fugue and recurring at frequent intervals, which may be considered as the musical core around which the composition is built.

Answer: the subject as heard in the second voice to enter. It is normally in the dominant key. Certain intervallic adjustments, to be explained later, may occur here.

---

[1] The words *voice, soprano, alto, tenor,* and *bass,* borrowed from vocal composition, are retained in instrumental fugues to identify melodic lines.

Countersubject: a contrasting melodic idea, comparable in length to the subject and consistently heard in counterpoint against the subject. There may be more than one countersubject or there may be none at all.

Episode: a passage, usually of several measures, during which the subject or answer is not heard in any voice. Episodes may occur within the exposition, but most frequently they are found at the beginning and the close of the middle section of the fugue. An episode, even though brief, should offer an appreciable contrast and some interest peculiar to itself. It may or may not be based on previous material.

Codetta: a term which has come to have a special meaning in a fugue. It is used mainly to define extensions and interpolations within the exposition, between the subject or answer as heard in one voice and the entrance of the next voice. However, it can and *should* be applied to short bridge passages anywhere in the fugue—even those of a single measure or less—which are too brief to be classed as episodes. This includes, in particular, *approaches to interior cadences* not involving the subject.

Stretto: any passage involving two or more (even the total number) of the voices in which the subject is treated canonically with a time interval shorter than the subject itself. A countersubject may also be treated in stretto, separately or in association with the subject.

THE SUBJECT

The first consideration in any fugue is the subject. Since not every melody is suitable for use in a fugue, what are the qualities of a good subject? Here we must deal with averages and ignore the exceptions. Judging by the preferences of the recognized masters, we may expect the following:

Brevity. Subjects of motive length are to be found. Phrases of four measures or less are frequent. The average length of subjects in Bach's *The Well-Tempered Clavier* is just under three measures, all meters considered equal.

Limited range. Successful fugues have been founded on subjects as narrow as a diminished fourth. (See *WTC*,[2] No. 4.) Ranges in excess of a ninth are exceptional. The average range of subject in *The Well-Tempered Clavier* is slightly less than an octave.

Distinctiveness. The subject should possess melodic and/or rhythmic characteristics which render it easy to follow even in inner voices.

Definite tonality. Since a subject is generally first heard in an unaccompanied single voice, it should be firmly based on the strong tones of the scale in order to establish the key quickly. It will be observed that many subjects move at once from the tonic to the dominant or in the reverse direction with few, if any, intervening tones. Such movement leaves no doubt as to the key or the position of the subject within the scale.

The points just mentioned are well illustrated in the subjects quoted below. To facilitate our study, the answers are given in each case and placed directly beneath their respective subjects for ready comparison. All quotations are from Bach's music, and all but one are from *The Well-Tempered Clavier.*

Example 142.   a   **WTC, v. I, No. 12**

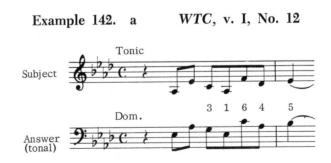

---

[2] *The Well-Tempered Clavier* will often be indicated in the following pages by *WTC*.

b   **Little Organ Fugue in G Minor**

c   *WTC*, v. I, No. 5

d   *WTC*, v. 2, No. 1

e   *WTC*, v. 2, No. 12

f   *WTC*, v. 1, No. 1

g   *WTC*, v. 1, No. 24

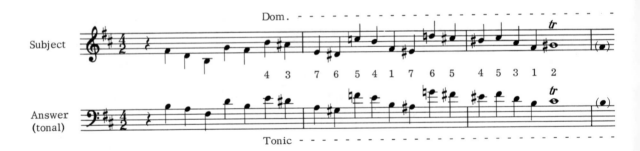

REAL AND TONAL ANSWERS

It will be noticed that a so-called "real" answer is a literal reproduction of the subject while a "tonal" answer is not. The changes which occur in the latter involve especially the tonic and dominant tones and are restricted almost invariably to the *beginning* of the answer. In this situation the tonic tone in the subject calls for the dominant tone in the answer and vice versa. After these changes the second voice proceeds quite in the manner of a real answer. In some instances only the first note is affected (see Example 142-*e*); such an answer is still, however, classified as tonal.

The reasons for such changes are alleged by some scholars to go back to the old church modes. Each of these modes had two forms, composed of the same tones but differing primarily in range. If the range was from final to final, or as we would say now, tonic to tonic, the form was called *authentic*.

If the range was from dominant to dominant it was called *plagal*. The "rule," according to this hypothesis, was that a theme for imitation presented in the lower or upper part of one form must be imitated in the corresponding part of the other form. Since the corresponding parts were unequal—thus:

—the imitation could not always be exact.

There are some objections to this explanation, even though it may have some historical basis. For one thing, real answers involving an initial jump of a fifth are to be found in sixteenth-century polyphony. Another and more important objection for our present purposes is that it does not satisfactorily explain Bach's frequent use of the tonal answer. He wrote in our present tonal system and was not subject to any ancient modal restrictions. In his fugues, and indeed in the great body of fugues generally, a much more plausible explanation may be deduced from the tendency of almost all subjects to end with some sense of cadence—not a conclusive cadence, to be sure, but with some degree of cadential inference. Unless the subject itself modulates, it will end on tonic harmony. Note how often Bach's subjects end on the mediant tone or the tonic. If the subject shows an initial leap from the tonic tone to the dominant, or vice versa, direct or with an intervening tone, the answer must be tonal if it enters (as it often does) while this tonic harmony, projected from the subject, is still in effect. The switch to the dominant key will follow.

Modulating subjects usually end in the dominant key. A real answer would move the key center to the supertonic. Since this is too far afield so early in the fugue, a tonal answer reestablishing the tonic key is virtually mandatory. (See *WTC*, v. 1, No. 24.)

Several tonal answers may be seen in Example 142. As just stated, the changes most conspicuously affect the tonic and dominant tones and are confined to the beginning of the answer. Notice that in Example 142-**a** only the first *e*-flat (dominant tone) of the subject is answered by the tonic *a*-flat. The *e*-flat in the second measure is answered by *b*-flat (dominant of E-flat). Similarly, in Example 142-**d**, the *g* in measure 2 of the subject is answered by *d* and not by the tonic *c* as in measure 1.

The switch to the *key* of the dominant in the answer is usually made immediately after the last tonal change.[3] The exact point can easily be discovered by determining where the notes of the tonic key, as sounded in the subject, are answered by the dominant counternotes in the second voice. This is demonstrated in Examples 142-**a**, -**d**, and -**e** by numerals indicating notes of the two scales. The numerals apply to subject and answer alike and begin at the point where the answer is definitely in the dominant.

An exceptional case is seen in Example 142-**g** where the subject, starting in B minor, modulates to the dominant. The answer, following standard procedure, performs a reverse modulation to the tonic. For practical analytical purposes this means that as much as possible of the subject should be considered to be in the dominant key and, conversely, as much as possible of the answer should be considered to be in the tonic key. The switch of keys takes place at the fourth beat of measure 1 of the subject. The numerals show the melodic and scalar agreement between dominant in the subject and tonic in the answer. Notice that *g*, the third beat of measure 1, is answered by *d*. This means that Bach regarded it as the submediant of B minor and answered it accordingly with *d* of the dominant. In other words, the switch has not yet taken place. The usual tonal changes account for the two *b*'s in measure 1 of the answer. A study of *The Well-Tempered Clavier* will show that a real answer is most likely where the subject moves along scale lines.

---

[3] The word *key* is emphasized in this sentence because the student must distinguish between the dominant *tone* which is merely the fifth of the scale and the dominant *key* which involves the sharping of the fourth tone of the tonic scale.

VOICES

It is often said that the exposition of a fugue is over when the last voice to enter has sounded the subject or answer, as the case may be. This is a dangerous assertion since the exceptions are many. Very often indeed there is an extra statement of the subject, usually by the first voice.

If there are three voices in the fugue, the normal thematic order in the exposition is subject–answer–subject. Additional voices continue the alternation: subject–answer–subject–answer–subject and so on. This means a constant oscillating between tonic and dominant tonalities.[4] Even a fourth statement in a three-voiced exposition is most likely to be in the dominant, as in the fugue appearing on the opposite page.

The order of entry of voices deserves some attention. There is no set pattern. If we consider all of Bach's fugues we find that he favored either the soprano or alto as the announcing voice. In *The Well-Tempered Clavier* fourteen fugues begin with the soprano, eighteen with the alto, seven with the tenor, and nine with the bass. After the first voice any conceivable order of the remaining voices may be adopted. These facts are only statistics and have no value in judging a fugue. However, the effectiveness of a strong bass entry after the fugue is underway cannot be denied. Bach must have felt this since he seldom, if ever, began an organ fugue in the bass (i.e., the pedals) and there is no technical reason why he could not have done so.

SELECTED ANALYTICAL STUDIES FROM *THE WELL-TEMPERED CLAVIER*

As an example of a perfectly constructed and exceptionally tuneful fugue, we have selected No. 21 from *The Well-Tempered Clavier*. There are two countersubjects, an unusual feature in so short a fugue. The exposition is "close," that is, the second and third entries occur immediately after the subject or answer is completed in the preceding voice. There is no codetta, nor is there any use of stretto anywhere. The soprano repeats the answer in the exposition beginning at measure 13.

The student should be reminded that an answer is the subject as first heard in the second voice to enter. It may or may not show tonal changes. But if there are such changes, it is advisable to refer to the answer *as* the answer wherever, throughout the fugue, this changed version occurs, to distinguish it from the original version as announced in the subject. In this particular fugue there is definitely a tonal answer (compare measure 5 with measure 1). In the middle section and again in the final section we find the "answer" version of the subject. In the middle section the subject is heard in G minor and is answered tonally in the subdominant, C minor. In the final section the subject returns in the key of E-flat and is answered tonally in B-flat, dominant of E-flat, but also the tonic key of the fugue as a whole. Thereafter the fugue remains in B-flat.[5] There is ample reason for a tonal answer in this fugue, quite apart from any ancient rule. If the student will examine every measure where the answer enters, he will see that the prevailing harmony precludes a real answer.

Some analysts would label the middle and final sections as "expositions 2 and 3," but this author prefers to limit the term "exposition" in a fugue, as in any other type of composition, to the opening section where the melodic material is first "exposed."

Wherever the subject or answer is sounded in this fugue, *both* countersubjects are heard in counterpoint. They appear in almost every possible combination. The subject, answer, and both countersubjects are heard in all the voices. Since there are three voices the fugue is said to be in *triple* counterpoint.

---

[4] Exceptions to this order in the *WTC* are:
    No. 1 (subject–answer–answer–subject)
    No. 12 (subject–answer–subject–subject)
    No. 14 (subject–answer–subject–subject),
with corresponding tonic or dominant tonalities.

[5] This relationship of subdominant (E-flat) to tonic (B-flat) in the final section is of course identical with tonic (B-flat) to dominant (F) in the exposition. Bach was using simple logic in ending his fugue as he did. It will be recalled that Schubert used this same key relationship in entering the recapitulation of his Fifth Symphony. (See p. 148.)

The fugue is presented in open score for greater clarity. Perhaps because of the greater maneuverability permitted by restricting the number of voices to three, Bach has used a subject with the unusually wide range of a minor tenth.

WTC, Fugue No. 21

A series of graphs in color has been provided later in this chapter, in which the form of the above fugue, as well as others to be considered presently, can be easily observed. The various contrapuntal combinations involving subjects and countersubjects are also made quite clear. In these graphs a black line represents the subject, a red line represents a first countersubject, and a green line represents a second countersubject. Consult Graph 1 now and verify all details by a comparison with the music on the preceding pages.

For Examples 143, 144, and 145, it will be necessary to see a copy of *The Well-Tempered Clavier*.

Example 143. *WTC*, Fugue No. 3 (Tonal with one countersubject)

The soprano repeats the answer in measures 10 and 11. This occurs after a short episode which occupies the position of a codetta. It is called an episode here because of the distinctive melodic material. The same material is used in other episodes later in the fugue. Measures 10 and 11 are included in the exposition: an episode within an exposition is by no means rare.

The long episode beginning in measure 29, separating the middle and final sections, is really in two parts, the division being at measure 35. This fugue has a clear recapitulation formed by the same order of voices and in the same keys that we heard in the exposition, except that the final statement in the soprano is in the tonic.

A small analytical problem arises at measure 21. We are approaching a cadence in E-sharp minor (measure 22). Thereafter the soprano continues with a motivic sequence (based on a fragment of the subject) preparatory to a restatement of the subject in G-sharp (measures 25–26). Measures 21–24 therefore are not a unit, certainly not an episode. They are analyzed here as two codettas, the first completing a phrase and the second being an interpolation. (See Graph 2.)

Example 144. *WTC*, Fugue No. 8 in E-Flat Minor (In some editions, D-sharp minor)
(Tonal without countersubject)

This fugue is regarded by many students of Bach as the best in *The Well-Tempered Clavier* collection. This is a matter of opinion, but there can be no disagreement about its status as a masterpiece of counterpoint—it is in a class by itself. Its short subject is heard almost constantly, often inverted and finally in augmentation. There is much use of stretto, which accounts in some degree for the absence of a countersubject. (See Graph 3.)

Example 145. *WTC*, Fugue No. 4 (Five voices, two countersubjects)

It is difficult to classify this fugue as either real or tonal. The first answer is real and in the dominant but the second (Alto I beginning at measure 12) is just as surely a tonal answer. The dominant tone, *g-sharp*, (measure 12) answers the tonic, *c-sharp*, in Alto II (measure 7) as to be expected, but thereafter this second answer is definitely in the *subdominant*. This use of both dominant and subdominant within the same exposition is unusual. Busoni and Riemann[6] agree that measures 22–35 constitute a second or counterexposition; however, it is incomplete. The soprano and first alto are concerned with free counterpoint only. The keys involved in the counterexposition are (in the order of entries) F-sharp, C-sharp, B, and E. That is to say, there is a modulation to the relative major of the original key.

There are two countersubjects but both are deferred until after the expositions. The first countersubject is used almost constantly, either by direct quotation or figurally, in the counterpoints, in measures 36 to 94. The varying lengths of the subject and two countersubjects are caused by augmentation or diminution of individual notes here and there or, in the countersubjects, by small extensions.

---

[6] See *The Well-Tempered Clavier*, Vol. I, Ferruccio B. Busoni, (Ed.), (New York, G. Schirmer, Inc.), p. 25 (footnote). Dr. Hugo Riemann (1849–1919), German scholar and theorist, is remembered for his analyses of Bach's works, including *J. S. Bachs Wohltemperirtes Clavier*, published by Augener Ltd., London.

The stretto (measures 94–100), involving both the subject and the second countersubject, should be especially studied.

There is no passage in this fugue that can positively be called an episode. The five measures from measure 84 through 88 are marked as an episode on our graph, but even this could be disputed. The great prominence Bach gives to the countersubjects creates this problem of analysis. After the counterexposition the subject (or answer) is heard nineteen times, the first countersubject is heard seventeen times (excluding run-on extensions), and the second countersubject thirty-one times. Because of this continuous activity any episode would include a countersubject.

Some writers are inclined to regard this work as a triple fugue. This view is weakened by the fact that neither countersubject is presented in a specific exposition of its own nor introduced simultaneously with the subject. It is, rather, a case of *deferred* countersubjects. (See Graph 4.) There are several bona fide codettas, all leading to interior cadences of various weights.

A sharp contrast to the last two fugues considered here may be seen in Bach's Organ Fugue in C-minor, in which there are fifty-one continuous measures without even a suggestion of the subject. The whole of this extended passage is given over to development.

The graphs are but a hint of the unlimited variety possible in pieces in fugal style. No fugue can be taken for granted: each must be analyzed separately to ascertain its individual formal characteristics, irrespective of its probable ternary base. There has been no attempt at exhaustiveness in our studies dealing with fugue. This is an area of composition that can be completely covered only in a specialized course. For this reason we have stopped short of double and triple fugues and other complicated types. As justification for limiting our objective in this chapter, it may be observed that most fugues are relatively uncomplicated and should cause the beginning analyst little trouble if he has conscientiously studied the definitions and graphs.

There is confusion sometimes, even among experts, about where a fugal subject ends. One should examine every statement of the subject throughout a given fugue to discover what the composer *consistently treated* as a subject or answer, and be guided accordingly. This is necessary only to establish a criterion at the exposition by which to judge subsequent appearances of a subject, that is, to know whether it has been changed or altered in any way.

In the great majority of expositions the subject is completed before the entry of the next voice, but there are rare instances of stretto even this early in a fugue (see *WTC*, Vol. II, No. 3).

SUGGESTED ASSIGNMENTS

1. List separately the tonal and real fugues of *The Well-Tempered Clavier*. Be prepared to explain any tonal answer.
2. Make graphs,[†] in the manner demonstrated in this chapter, of fugues selected from the following lists:

The Well-Tempered Clavier
Vol. I: 1, 2, 6, 7, 9, 10, 11, 15, 16, 17
Vol. II: 1, 2, 7, 8, 12, 15

[†] The use of colored crayons in the preparation of graphs is strongly recommended.

Graph 1. *WTC*, Fugue No. 21

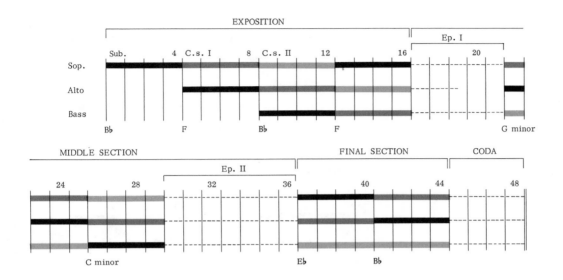

Graph 2. *WTC*, Fugue No. 3

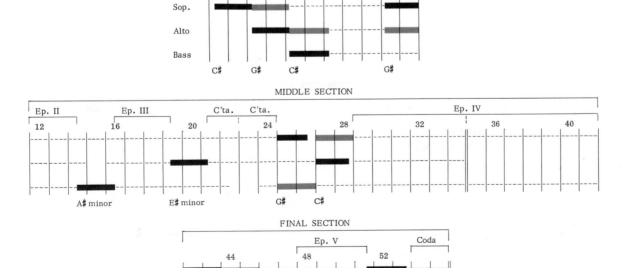

Graph 3.

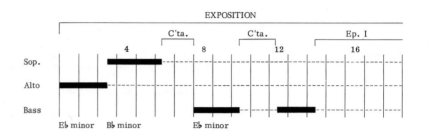

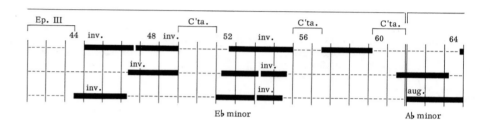

Graph 4.

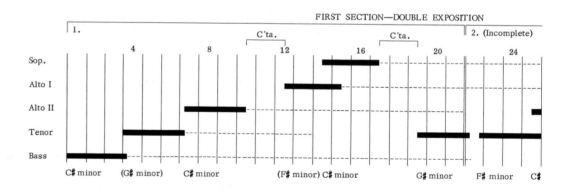

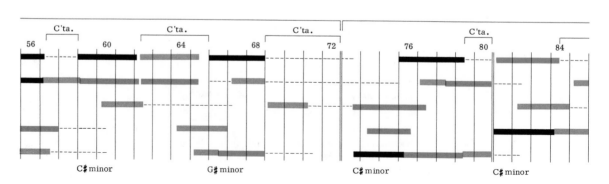

WTC, Fugue No. 8

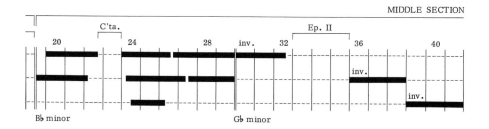

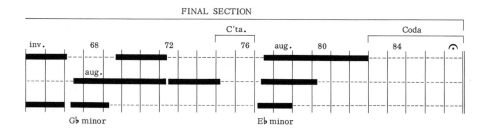

WTC, Fugue No. 4

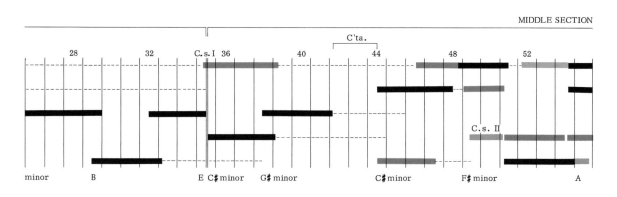

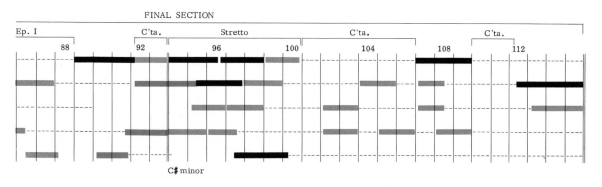

12

Miscellaneous Studies

In the previous nine chapters we have confined our attention to the standard or common musical forms, from the single-period or unipartite piece, to the symphony and the fugue. Only in the chapter on canon were we concerned with technique rather than formal design itself. It is scarcely necessary to add that this does not end a study of form in music. Any practicing musician or, for that matter, any listener with an analytical ear will become aware that many compositions, including some of the best-known ones, do not fit into any general category. Indeed, such a composition may stand alone as the only one of its kind.

This chapter deals with works which are either unique in form or present an unusual treatment of an old form. There is a wealth of music of acknowledged merit from which to make our selection.

HYBRID FORMS

When Chopin ventured beyond the simple ternary form in which he cast most of his compositions, the result was often something that did not fit into any of the classical forms. In his time this freedom called forth some unfavorable criticism. But content, not form, determines whether a composition lives or suffers an early demise. Chopin's four ballades for piano are among the world's most played music.[1] Their form therefore is of more than incidental interest.

No two of the ballades are alike in form but all show certain common features such as the compound duple meter (6/8 or 6/4), the unusual length as compared to most other instrumental ballades, and the variety of themes. Graphs are given for the first and fourth.

If we eliminate the coda, transitions, and bridges, the graph for Example 146 can be charted linearly as *A–B–A–B–C–B–A*. The rondo influence is obvious. But the first and second themes are both heard three times. Ignoring, for the moment, changes of key, the design by letters could be compressed to $\|: A\text{--}B :\| C\text{--}B\text{--}A$. Compare this with the design of the first movement of Mozart's Piano Sonata, K. 311 (Example 110), where it was seen that the positions of the first and second themes were reversed in the recapitulation. One may see, then, resemblances to both the rondo and sonata-form. Yet this ballade is neither a rondo nor a sonata, nor is it a sonata-rondo. Further complicating factors are the frequent and brilliant transitions and the brevity of the first theme in its second and third appearances, in which it is quickly dissolved, leaving the theme with little more than the effect of a transition itself.

---

[1] The vocal ballade, or ballad, is a song which tells a story; there is little, if any, such meaning attached to instrumental ballades, however. The title has also been used by other romantic composers such as Liszt, Brahms and Grieg. None of these pieces, including those of Chopin, appears to have been written with any definite programmatic intent. In form, the ballades of Brahms are simple ternary, while Grieg's Ballade in G minor, an excellent piano number, is a theme with variations.

Similarities to the old standard forms are inevitable in any extended piece that is constructed on a repetitive plan. Nevertheless, the form of this ballade is unique and must be classed as a hybrid.

The choice of keys is equally unorthodox. No theme is in the dominant—after the tonic itself, the submediant is the most used key; indeed, if the body of the composition alone is considered (that is, without the coda), the submediant replaces the tonic as the favored key. The remote key of E is arrived at by the most natural of melodic means after the return of the first theme (A[2]) in A minor.

Example 146.   Chopin, Ballade in G Minor, Opus 23

Intro. (8)

$$
\begin{array}{c}
A \\
\hline
\text{First Th. (27)} \\
\text{G minor}
\end{array}
\quad \text{C'ta. (12)} \quad \text{T. (20)} \rightarrow
\quad
\begin{array}{c}
B \\
\text{Second Th.} \\
\hline
a(15) \ \ b(11) \\
\text{E}\flat
\end{array}
\rightarrow
$$

$$
\begin{array}{c}
A^2 \\
\hline
\text{First Th. (12)} \rightarrow \\
\text{A minor}
\end{array}
\quad
\begin{array}{c}
B^2 \\
\hline
\text{Second Th. (12+8)} \rightarrow \\
\text{A}
\end{array}
\text{T. (12)}
$$

$$
\begin{array}{c}
C \\
\hline
\text{Ep. (12)} \\
\text{E}\flat
\end{array}
\quad \text{T. (8+8)} \rightarrow
\quad
\begin{array}{c}
B^3 \\
\text{Second Th.} \rightarrow \\
\hline
a(15) \ \ b(13) \\
\text{E}\flat
\end{array}
$$

$$
\begin{array}{c}
A^3 \\
\hline
\text{First Th. (12+2)} \\
\text{G minor}
\end{array}
\quad
\begin{array}{c}
\text{Coda} \\
\hline
\text{Sec. I (8) Sec. II (35) Sec. III (14)} \\
\text{G minor}
\end{array}
$$

The following ballade is nearer to sonata-form than the one in G minor and the graph (using dotted lines) is fashioned accordingly. However, this analysis is offered only as a guide for comparison. The form is too free to pass as an example of sonata-form. The primary theme is heard in two variations of the type referred to as "doubles" in Chapter 7. This amounts to saying that the techniques used are ornamental rather than structural. The recapitulation begins with a reappearance of the short introduction, this time in A. The primary theme follows in D minor. Compare with C to F minor at the beginning. The stormy coda is a tour de force, independent of previous themes.

Example 147.   Chopin, Ballade in F Minor, Opus 52

Exposition[2]

Intro. (7)   Pr.   Th. (29)   Br. (1)   Ep. (8+12)
C   F minor A♭   G♭ MOD.

$$
\begin{array}{c}
\text{Pr.} \qquad \text{Th. (14)} \quad \text{T. (8)} \quad \text{Sub. Th. (20)} \\
\text{F minor A}\flat \qquad\qquad\qquad\quad \text{B}\flat \\
\hline
\text{Var. I}
\end{array}
$$

Middle Theme

Sec. I (8) Sec. II (14) Sec. III (7)

[2] The terms "exposition" and "recapitulation" are applicable to any ternary-based composition in which the principal themes are introduced in the first part and repeated (at least partially) in the third part.

Recapitulation

```
Intro. (5+1)    Pr.      Th.      (34)    Sub. Th. (22)
A                   D minor  F minor  Ab      Db
                    ─────────────────────
                             Var. 2
```

```
              Coda
Sec. I (4+8+8) Sec. II (16) Sec. III (13)
F minor  .   .   .   .   .
```

UNUSUAL ADAPTATIONS OF CLASSICAL FORMS

Chopin's four scherzos for piano solo were conceived on a grand scale that far removes them from all comparison to the usual trifle found among the movements of a sonata. As a group they afford the analyst an excellent opportunity to study this composer's uninhibited use of form. This free spirit was surely at work during the writing of the second scherzo where we find the exposition to be longer than the combined length of the rest of the piece by over a hundred measures.

If we consider the thematic material without repetitions, the exposition extends through 206 measures. In performance this amounts to 412 measures since the repetitions are written out and are therefore mandatory. The exposition is in two major divisions, which are in two and three parts respectively. The tranquil pace of subpart *a* of the second division, immediately following the preceding turbulence, suggests the primary-subordinate contrasting of themes in many sonatas, but the resemblance goes no further than this momentary change of mood. It is for this reason that the word "theme" has been avoided here. There are grounds for regarding the divisions as a first and second exposition, but that might lead to confusion with the classical double exposition, which was a different thing entirely. Both divisions are cadenced and each is repeated separately.

An eight-measure transition takes us into the development. There need be no hesitancy about terminology at this point. No composition ever had a more authentic development. The materials are drawn from both divisions of the exposition. In method and spirit there is a striking similarity to the same composer's Sonata in B-flat minor.

The second division of the exposition is not heard in the recapitulation. Compare this procedure with the much more frequent omission of the *first* theme in sonatas.

Example 148.   Chopin, Scherzo in B-Flat Minor, Opus 31

Exposition (A)

```
        Division I                              Division II
‖: a(48+16) → b(53)  C'ta. (15) :‖: a(20 |2da 21| +25) b(24) → c(32) :‖   T. (8)
 Bb minor Db      Db                  A                   C# minor E
```

```
              Development (B)
Sec. I (16) Sec. II (25) Sec. III (18) Sec. IV (9) Sec. V (40)
```

```
Recapitulation (A)
     Division I                            Coda
a(48+16) → b(60)  C'ta. (8)     Sec. (8) Sec. II (32) Sec. III (25)
Bb minor Db   Db                 A                  Db
```

Example 149.   Schumann, *Carnaval*, Opus 9

This work, a concert favorite, consists of eighteen short pieces, plus an introduction (préambule) and a finale. According to reliable sources, Schumann wrote these pieces one at a time with no particular purpose in mind and later assembled them into a series.

The word *carnaval* is French for carnival. Schumann seems to have had in mind something in the nature of a *mardi gras*. We need not be concerned with the whimsical titles ("Florestan," "Coquette," "Pierrot" and so on) attached to the individual pieces, other than to remark that our composer was following the example of Couperin and other earlier musicians in this practice. The comparison to Couperin is apt on another count. This prolonged fantasy is more related to the *ordres* of the French master than it is to a suite. It is a collection of pieces put together rather freely but intended for continuous performance.

Schumann describes the work as *scènes mignonnes sur quartre notes* (little scenes on four notes). He is referring to a small figuration or motive of four notes (sometimes three) which starts off almost every piece or "scene." This leads us to a curious facet of this great romanticist's genius, his remarkable ability to create a series of independent melodies, all beginning with a common motive. We meet it again in his *Symphonic Studies*, Opus 13, and in the Concerto in A minor.[3]

In the *Symphonic Studies* the motive is:

In the Concerto in A minor it is:

In the *Carnaval* it happens to be:

or (variant)

As the Germans spell the scale these notes represent the letters A–S($e\flat$)–C–H(b) or AS($a\flat$)–C–H, which, arranged as S–C–H–A, disclose that Schumann, with his own name obviously in mind, was playing an old musical letters game that even Bach indulged in on occasion.

These pieces have been described as "variations" by some writers. Schumann himself made no such claim though it seems that he did intend certain of the *Symphonic Studies* as variations. If we concur in this opinion, then we must regard the first movement of the concerto as a series of interrupted variations. A more accurate view is that these works are variations in the *use of a motive*. This sets them apart from variations on a *theme*.

A graph of this work, to be completed by the student, will be found on page 216.

Example 150.   Franck, Symphony in D Minor, Third Movement

The first movement of Franck's Symphony in D minor came before us in an earlier chapter (see graph, p. 150.) The work as a whole should be studied because it is an outstanding example of the cyclic technique of welding together an extended composition in several movements by the transference of themes.

In Franck's symphony this process is cumulative. Themes from the first and second movements are woven into the third and final movement. The last movement is in abbreviated sonata-form.

A graph of the third movement, to be completed by the student, will be found on page 217.

---

[3] The student will appreciate this statement more if he will examine the Concerto in A minor where he will find, in the first movement, that the principal theme, the subordinate theme, and two themes in the middle sections (development) all begin in an identical manner but continue along independent courses after the first four notes.

César Franck's *Symphonic Variations* is a most successful union of piano and orchestra. As a concert number it is the equivalent of a concerto, affording the soloist ample opportunity to display his talents both as a musician and a performer. The form can be summarized as a set of continuous variations based on two themes with three general groupings suggesting the movements of a symphony.

Franck does not at first present his themes as complete statements. His manner of allowing a theme to grow from a motivic source reminds one of Schumann. At the very beginning the orchestra sounds a phrase which foreshadows one of the principal themes. Because of the position of this phrase the theme (heard later) is designated as Theme I. After four measures the first phrase of Theme II is heard in the piano. The following quotations are representative:

Franck was not interested here in sectionalized variations, nor in conventional variations on a theme in any strict sense. He favored the *thème varié* concept, which is more concerned with related themes growing from a common source. This explains the inequality of length among the variations and the frequent changes in the melodic line.

Vincent d'Indy, the most famous pupil of César Franck, regarded the first 115 measures as introductory. This view has met with some minor disagreement among more distant observers of French music, but it is substantially adopted here, not only because of its distinguished backing but also because it simplifies the problem of analysis. Within these 115 measures, which together complete a ternary formation, both themes emerge in distinct and fully developed versions. Both are played by the piano unaccompanied. In other sections there is a good deal of dialogue between orchestra and soloist. (See Example 76 for a complete version of Theme I.)

There are elements of both themes in several of the variations. (See measures 56–57, which occur within the first complete version of Theme I.) But these cross references are secondary. Always one theme or the other will dominate in a given variation. As will be seen in the graph,[4] the two themes are not alternated in regular order.

Example 151. Franck, *Symphonic Variations*

First Movement (*Poco allegro*)

Introduction _____

	A(1–46)			B(47–63)	A²(64–116)			
	a(16) *b*(16) *c*(14)			Th. I (Piano)	*b*(14)	*a*(13)	T. (8)	*c*(18)
	Th's I & II Th. I				Pts reversed			Th. I
	F♯ minor A minor A			C♯ minor E	G (Mod.)	C♯		F♯ minor

[4] Numerals in brackets after small letters (subparts) are measure totals. Other numerals represent specific measures.

Variations begin.

Var. 1 (Th. I)	Var. 2 (Th. I)	Var. 3 (Th. I)
117–139	140–157	158–170
F♯ minor	F♯ minor	F♯ minor

    (A)   (B)   (A²)

Var. 4 (Th. I)	Var. 5 (Th's. I & II)	Br. (207–208)	Var. 6 (Th. I)
171–186	187–206		209–228
	a(8) b(12)		
D B	(D♯) (B) E minor		D F♯ minor

Second Movement (*Molto più lento*)

Var. 7 (Th. I)	Var. 8 (Th. II)	Ext. and Br. (284–289)
229–248	249–283	
F♯	F♯ minor	

Third Movement (*Allegro non troppo*)
(In sonata-form)

Exposition

Var. 9 (Th. II)	Var. 10 (Free)	Br. (319–320)
290–305	306–318	
F♯	C♯	

                                                  quasi Sub. Th.

Var. 11 (Th. II)	Tutti (333–336)	Var. 12 (Th. I) (337–354)	
321–332	Transition based on Th. II	a(8)	b(10)
F♯	(Mod.) D	D F	F D

                          quasi Middle Th.

Tutti (355–366)	Var. 13 (Th. II)
Based on Th. II	367–384
	E♭

Variation 13 provides the necessary break between exposition and recapitulation. It is played by the piano alone and is the nearest approach to a cadenza to be found in this work.

Recapitulation

Var. 14 (Th. II)	Br. (406–410)	Var. 15 (Th. II)
385–405		(411–422)
(Mod.) F♯		Same as Var. 11
		F♯

Var. 16 (Th. I) (423–441)		Coda (442–462)
a(8)	b(11)	
Same as Var. 12		
F♯ C♯ F♯		F♯

In Variations 12 and 16, analyzed here as the subordinate theme, the melody in the piano is not derived from either of the principal themes, but the accompaniment (orchestra) definitely recalls Theme I. Both variations are in two parts. Variation 10 is marked "free" because it is so great a departure that it can be regarded as a new theme despite certain remote derivations here and there.

Thematic relationships set up a ternary block involving Variations 4, 5, and 6. This has been suggested in the graph. This, as well as thematic constructions throughout, should be studied thoroughly.

Franz Liszt's Sonata in B minor is his most ambitious work for piano and probably his most important. On its publication in 1854 it was greeted by a storm of abuse, and there are critics who continue to regard it as controversial. But after more than a century it is still a concert favorite.

Liszt's conception was revolutionary. He expanded the three major divisions of the one-movement sonata-form into what amounts to three "movements," thus:

> First movement: Exposition
> Second movement: Middle theme
> Third movement: Recapitulation.

The sonata has been variously analyzed as one, three, or even four movements, depending on one's point of view. The purists will regard it as a single movement because the thematic scheme of the one-movement form is preserved even though it is widely dispersed and at times becomes well-nigh lost in the numerous flights of virtuosity. The fact that the movements are played without pause decides nothing, for movements, even in Beethoven's music, are frequently fused. The claim for four movements rests on the thin argument that the very brief fugatto at the beginning of the movement of recapitulation constitutes a separate movement. For convenience and simplicity this author will treat the sonata as a work in three movements.

Although Liszt claimed that he would "break the bonds of sonata-form," he retained certain traditional features of the form. There is a primary theme in the tonic minor and a subordinate theme in the relative major. Both reappear intact in the third movement (recapitulation) in proper order, but with the subordinate theme in the tonic major. In classifying sections—so unprecedented is this music—the author has been guided by those sections or themes which have unmistakable credentials in classical sonata-form and has labelled intervening sections or passages accordingly.

Quotations used in the analysis are according to the Peters Edition. Notice that the numerals are *measure numbers* and not measure totals. Encircled numerals show measure numbers of the quoted passages in the score. In a few instances these do not coincide with the first measure of the part in which these passages occur.

The whole sonata is based on a few very short motives, the most important of which are quoted below. The second movement is marked by the announcement of a new and song-like melody unrelated to any previous material. This lack of a regular development is more than offset by the composer's almost constant manipulation of his motives throughout the entire remainder of the work. Some of the myriad ways in which these motives are used may be seen in the few quotations, but only after a complete study of the whole sonata can Liszt's incredible inventiveness in the use of such meager materials be even surmised.

Example 152. Liszt, Sonata in B Minor[5]

First Movement (A) (quasi exposition)

Introduction (1–32)

Principal motives
(First appearance)

(1-3)

p. 1   Principal motive 1

(9-10)

Principal motive 2

[5] Issued singly or in album by Peters. Pages numbered here from first page of music.

(14-15)

Principal motive 3

Primary Theme (32–54)

Allegro energico

p. 2 ③②

etc.

T.

Sec. I (55–81) Sec. II (82–104)

Subordinate Theme

Part I (105-119)

Grandioso

p. 6 ⑩⑤   Secondary motive

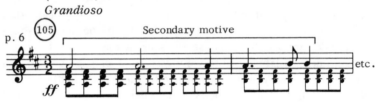

etc.

Transition (120-152)

Dolce con grazia

p. 6 ①②⑤

etc.

Part II (153-197)

Cantando espressivo

p. 7 ①⑤③

etc.

Transition (197–204)

Episode
(not in third movement)

Section I (205-238)

p. 10 ②⑩⑤   8va - - - ┐

Section II (239-254)

Coda

Codetta I (255-276)

Codetta II (277-285)

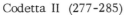

Codetta III (286-296)

T.

Sec. I (297–318) Sec. II (319–330)

Second Movement (B) (simple ternary)

First Theme (a) (331–347) F♯–C♯

Second Theme (b)

Part I (340-362)

Part II (363-394)   Actually a variant of Part I of the subordinate theme.

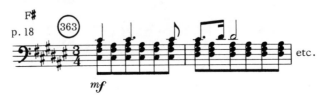

First Theme (a²) (395–413) F♯

Transition (413–452)

Third Movement (A²) (quasi recapitulation)

Introduction (453–459). This is as at first, but transposed.
Fugato (460–505) B♭ minor

Later

The fugato passes into a long transitional passage built exclusively on Motives 2 and 3. In measures 509 and 510 may be seen Motive 2 inverted in the bass, in counterpoint with an elaborate and somewhat contracted chordal version of itself in the treble.

Transition (506-532)

Primary Theme (533–555) (B minor). This is substantially as found in first movement.

$$\frac{\text{T. (Pages 25–27)}}{\text{Sec. I (555–565) Sec. II (566–581) Sec. III (582–599)}}$$

Although founded on the same motivic material, this long transition differs much from that in the corresponding position in the first movement.

Subordinate Theme

Part I (600-615)

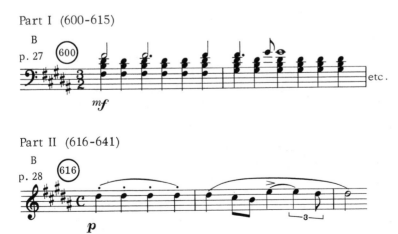

Part II (616-641)

Transition (642–649)

The sonata is brought to a close by an extensive coda which can be subdivided into seven codettas.

Codetta I (650–672). This is as found at first.

Codetta II (673-681)

Codetta III (682-699)

Codetta IV (700-710)

Codetta V (711-728)

Codetta VI (729-749) Motive used as ostinato bass.

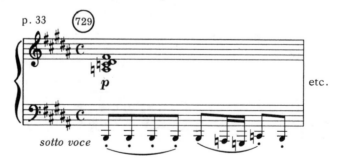

Codetta VII (750-760)

In this long coda Liszt sums up his sonata, even to recalling the first theme of the second move-ment, which is not based on any previous motive. As anyone who has taken the trouble to listen to this sonata will agree, the composer has, long before arriving at this coda, used his motives in almost every possible way, both in the mechanics of variation and in those of mood.

Good recordings of this sonata are always to be had. Before listening to an uninterrupted per-formance, the student should be familiar with all the principal motives. It would be a great additional aid, if a piano is at hand in the classroom, to play several times and slowly the material in measures 32–43 (at least the right hand part), measures 106–115, measures 154–160, and measures 256–263. This would give the class something for the ear and the mind to anchor on when hearing the entire work.

A vast amount of music, including some of the most revered masterpieces, exists behind a few much-used generic titles. Three such titles are brought to attention below, along with recommendations of specific compositions for the student's further investigation.

THE STUDY, OR ÉTUDE

Most studies are written for the purpose of developing facility in performance, but a sufficient number have been written by musicians, as distinct from technicians, to justify a look into this corner of the literature. One thinks at once of the twenty-four studies by Chopin and their enduring popularity in the concert hall. But Chopin's studies are all based on the simple ternary design and are not ap-propriate material for discussion at this point.

This cannot be said of several of the longer and more involved studies by Franz Liszt. These studies do not follow any set formal pattern, just as they do not deal exclusively with selected mechani-cal problems. At time goes on, it is increasingly evident that certain of these studies will probably outlast all of Liszt's other writing. In addition to their extraordinary musical qualities, they well illus-trate this composer's flexibility in adapting old musical forms.

TOCCATAS

Pieces published under the title *toccata* abound in a variety of forms. The word itself comes from the Italian *toccare*, to touch. (Compare the French *toucher* and the Spanish *tocar*.) In a musical sense this means to *play* an instrument, most especially one with a keyboard. The organ and the piano have enjoyed an almost complete monopoly of the world's toccatas. As a genre these pieces have always been more or less associated with the display of virtuosity. The toccatas of Frescobaldi, Scheidt, Buxtehude, and Pachelbel show the prevailing dependence on massed chords and rapid scale passages.

A second and more complex type is credited to Johann Froberger (d. 1667) who introduced movements in fugal style. Bach followed this course, bringing the multi-movement toccata to a high state of perfection in his six toccatas for harpsichord. These works, which bear some features in common with the suite, are still in great favor with pianists. Some of the polyphonic movements are best described as fugatos, but there are several authentic fugues. For variety Bach's First Toccata (D major) is the most interesting. The movements are: prelude–fugato–adagio–double fugue (that is, two subjects announced simultaneously)–interlude (recalling the prelude)–fugue *alla giga.*

Since the days of Carl Czerny (1791–1857), toccatas for piano solo have become more and more pyrotechnical displays, written usually in continuous sixteenth notes featuring a steady but rapid tempo (*moto perpetuo*) from beginning to end. In the twentieth century, composers of such ·works have mercilessly exploited the percussive possibilities of the piano.

FANTASIES

There is no standard form for a fantasy, or fantasia. The title is used for pieces in one or several movements. Throughout the nineteenth century, virtuosi of both the violin and the piano wrote hundreds of potpourris on operatic or other tunes, most of which were known as fantasies. In more serious music the word has generally indicated a measure of unusual freedom in the use of form.

SUGGESTED ASSIGNMENTS

1. The graph below, of Schumann's *Carnaval,* Opus 9, is to be completed by the student. Copy it on a separate sheet, then complete it by adding graphs of the missing pieces, writing in titles above and the corresponding versions of the motive below.
   Indicate the key in every case.
   The motive has a greater formative influence in some of the pieces than in others. Be prepared to discuss this matter and substantiate your findings. The exaggerated augmentations of the motive entitled "Sphinxes," found in some editions, should be observed, but do not attempt to include them in the graphed outline.
   Complete an analysis of the finale, using the analysis of the preamble as a model.
   Carefully note all means that Schumann has used to secure unity in the work as a whole, with special attention to the preamble and finale.

   The preamble is a series of sections of varied lengths and coherencies. Only the first section is in the nature of a true preamble, that is, music in measured time as to suggest walking. Some of the sections break down into subsections as indicated in the divided measure counts. Notice that the first section is in ternary form, as are most of the little scenes which follow.

Préambule

Sec. I	Sec. II	Sec. III
‖: $a(6)$:‖ $b(8) \rightarrow a^2(10)$ ‖	(3) 8+7	(12)
A♭	A♭	E♭

Sec. IV	Sec. V	Coda (26)
8+16	8+8+15+12	A♭
A♭	C minor E♭ A♭	

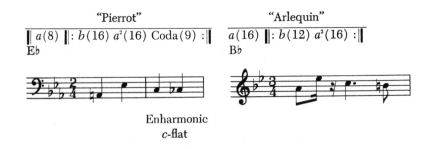

"Pierrot"	"Arlequin"
‖ $a(8)$ ‖: $b(16)$ $a^2(16)$ Coda(9) :‖	$a(16)$ ‖: $b(12)$ $a^2(16)$:‖
E♭	B♭

Enharmonic
c-flat

2. The next graph is Franck's Symphony in D Minor, Third Movement.

Introduction (6)

Pr. Th.

Exposition (A)
$$\overline{a(12) \rightarrow b(8+10) \rightarrow a^2(12)\ b^2(8+8)} \rightarrow T.(7)$$
$$\text{Sub. Th. } (8+8+10) \rightarrow \text{C'ta. } (12+15)\ \underline{\text{C'ta. } (8+8)} \rightarrow$$
$$?$$

Development (B)
$$\text{Sec. I } (8+12+8+8+10) \rightarrow \text{Sec. II } (8+8+9) \rightarrow$$
$$\underline{\text{Sec. III } (8+8)} \rightarrow \underline{\text{Sec. IV } (8+10)} \rightarrow \underline{\text{Sec. V } (8+14)} \rightarrow$$
$$\quad\quad ? \quad\quad\quad\quad\quad ? \quad\quad\quad\quad\quad ?$$

Pr. Th.

Recapitulation (A²) $\overline{a(12)\ b(8+12)}$ Sub. Th. and C'tas. omitted

Coda
$$\text{Sec. I } (18)\ \text{Sec. II } (12)\ \underline{\text{Sec. III } (8+8+4)} \rightarrow$$
$$?$$
$$\underline{\text{Sec. IV } (6+16+14+12)} \rightarrow \underline{\text{Sec. V } (12+31)}$$
$$\quad\quad\quad ? \quad\quad\quad\quad\quad\quad ?$$

First, listen to a recording with a score in hand. Copy from the score the principal themes of all three movements. (Most of them are short.) Be prepared to indicate which themes from the first and second movements are heard in the third movement and precisely where a particular theme is used. Be alert for evidences of thematic fragmentation and the combining of elements from two themes, either linearly or contrapuntally.

The lines and question marks under certain sections in the graph above indicate that thematic material from previous movements is used. Ascertain what themes are repeated, from which movement they are borrowed, and their original position within the form of that movement. The divisions in measure totals, as in most of the previous graphs, do not represent single phrases but phrase-groups, often with extensions.

3. Do not be frightened by the bristling notation of the suggested studies nor fooled by changes of key. Ferret out the melodies and make your conclusions accordingly. Work toward simplicity. The first study is graphed as a model.

Liszt, "Gnomenreigen" (Dance of the Gnomes), *Concert Étude*

A

$$\overline{\text{Intro. (4) } a(16)\ b(16)\ \text{Intro. (4) } a^2(16)\ b^2(20)}$$
$$\text{F\# minor A} \quad\quad\quad\quad\quad \text{F\# minor B}\flat$$

B(26)
G minor

A²

$$\overline{a^3(18)\ b^3(23)}\quad \text{Coda (25)}$$
$$\text{F\# minor F\#} \qu. \quad . \quad . \quad . \quad .$$

Part A includes a written-out repeat of subparts a and b. The repetition of subpart b (i.e., b²) is put in the unlikely key of B-flat. The basic form of the study is simple ternary.

4. Analyze the following studies by Liszt:

La Campanella

Concert Étude in D-flat (Un Sospiro)

Concert Étude in F minor, (A fascinating study in variations)

"Feux follets" (Will-o'-the-wisp) and "Mazeppa" from *Twelve Transcendental Studies*.

Notice the cyclic features in the last study. Is it a series of variations? Perhaps a rondo? Or both?

5. Among the best of piano toccatas are:
    Toccata, Opus 7, Schumann
    Toccata from the Suite *Pour le piano,* Debussy
    Toccata from the Suite *Tombeau de Couperin,* Ravel
    Toccata, Prokofieff
    All these pieces are worthwhile studies in form.
    It should be pointed out that many of Bach's short preludes are actually toccatas. See Preludes 2, 3, 5, 6, 11, and 20, among many others, from *The Well-Tempered Clavier.* The same could be said for numerous gigues, rondos, and prestos of the baroque and classical eras. A prime example is the third movement of Beethoven's piano sonata, Opus 10, No. 2.

6. Beethoven's Sonatas, Opus 27, Nos. 1 and 2, are called *quasi fantasias* because of certain liberties taken in the first movements. Study these movements and explain what liberties were taken.
    Other fantasies suitable for study are:
    Fantasy in C minor, Bach
    Fantasy (from the Chromatic Fantasy and Fugue), Bach
    (This piece is in sections. Determine the number of sections and the measure count of each.)
    Fantasy in C, Haydn
    Fantasy in F minor, Chopin
    (Construct a graph of this piece. Also, explain any logical reasons for its being called a fantasy.)
    Fantasy in C, Schumann (three movements)
    (The most distinguished of all romantic fantasies, well worth detailed study.)

13

Music from the Twentieth Century

The easy expression "twentieth century" as applied to music has been much abused. Too often it is made the private reserve of the avant-garde of the moment. It is pertinent to recall that whole schools of composition, such as impressionism, have reached their peak and waned since 1900. Such distinguished musicians as Sibelius and Rachmaninoff, who stood aside from the revolutionary movements about them, cannot be banished to the nineteenth century because they were conservatives. However, we will deal in this chapter with composers who are indisputably "twentieth century," all of whom have been in some degree associated with those singular changes and concepts which have so profoundly affected music in our day.

Some of this music will be found in the five works partially analyzed in the next pages. All of these works are long, consisting of several movements, sections, or independent pieces. External form will not be neglected, but greater emphasis will be placed on specific techniques and procedures. Since the latter cannot be disassociated from form, such studies have a place in the present book.

BARTÓK

Motives in Recent Composition

Example 153.   Bartók, String Quartet No. 5[1]

In his later years Béla Bartók became increasingly interested in achieving a perfect synthesis among the movements of a composition. To this end he placed great dependence on motivic development and the exploitation of selected intervals. In his Fourth and Fifth String Quartets he combined these techniques, with thematic integration of the movements, into what had long before become known as the "arch" pattern. (For an earlier use of the "arch" idea, as applied to a single movement, see Example 110.) We have seen what Liszt accomplished with a few motives. Bartók's special contribution was to refine the procedure. His methods were more subtle and were pursued with such persistence that it can be said that he rarely wrote anything that did not lead a bit farther toward a definite architectonic goal.

---

[1] Copyright 1936 by Universal Edition (London); renewed 1963. Copyright & renewal assigned to Boosey and Hawkes Inc. for the U.S.A. Excerpts reprinted by permission.

Let us consider briefly his Fifth String Quartet. A complete analysis of this work would require more space than can be afforded here, but some conception of its construction can be imparted by the following graph with a few words of direction and explanation.

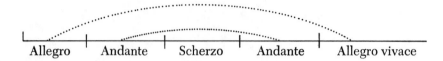

There are very obvious motivic bonds between the first and fifth movements and again between the second and fourth. For example, the opening repeated notes of the first movement

may be found again in the fifth movement (measures 662 through 685).

The motive

of the coda (*Allegro molto*) of the first movement becomes the most prolific source motive for the fifth movement. As in all displays of this technique, the motive undergoes constant changes, such as inversion, expansion or contraction, thus:

In the second movement at measure 31, we hear:

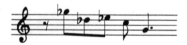

which may be found in the fourth movement as:

A short motive of the second movement

is expanded in the fourth movement to:

The third movement should not be neglected. Note the similarity of this motive found in the first movement:

to this one in the trio of the third movement:

Some of the motives may be identified as common to all movements.

This study can be properly completed only by listening to a performance or a recording, supplemented by a concentrated study of the score. Follow this with a like study of Bartók's Fourth String Quartet. In his sixth may be seen an example of an entire work growing out of a single theme; this theme is to be found at the beginning of every movement.

KŘENEK

Example 154.   Křenek, Twelve Short Pieces for Piano, Opus 83²

Ernst Křenek was one of the first important composers to adopt the dodecaphonic principles of Schoenberg and has written many works in the serial technique. For all the reputed complexity of his music, his Opus 83 offers a comparatively easy approach to studies of the tone-row system of composition. We have already met such a work by Webern in Chapter 10 (Example 141). At that point we were concerned primarily with a passage as a canon. It is now appropriate to look further into the structure of music written in what has come to be known as "classical" serialism.

Serialism

All such music originates with the adoption of some consecutive arrangement of the twelve tones called a row or series or, as the Germans say, *grundgestalt*. Several facts should be known before we proceed. A row may be used in any or all of four possible orders—the original row, its inversion, the retrograde or backward form, and the inversion of the retrograde. A typical row, as pictured in a textbook, is nothing but a series of notes, probably breves, in as near a straight line as possible. It is not a theme in itself but is, somewhat like a scale, the raw material from which themes and harmonies may be extracted. The tones may be assigned any time value, be shifted to any register, or be shared by several voices. Tones may be repeated either immediately, that is, in their normal place in the row, or, as we will see in Křenek's work, later. Any number of tones may be repeated as a unit, and occasionally a tone may be dropped. Křenek's little pieces are completely serial, without "foreign" or non-serial elements, as in free serialism. Furthermore, there are no transpositions to complicate analysis.

The pieces range from the transparently simple to the complex. Be alert for enharmonic spellings—a *b*-flat, for instance, is not disqualified for appearing as *a*-sharp. Inasmuch as common tones at identical points in two rows are to be found, it will happen that a tone here or there may do double service.

² Copyright 1939 by G. Schirmer, Inc., New York. Used by permission.

The four rows in Křenek's Opus 83 are given below. (Note abbreviations.)

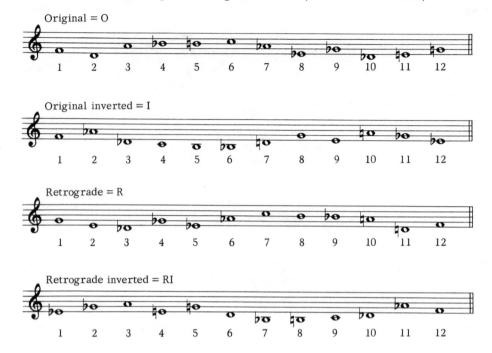

The original row is used alone in Opus 83, No. 1:

The inverted form is used in No. 2 (quote is from measures 8, 9, and 10):

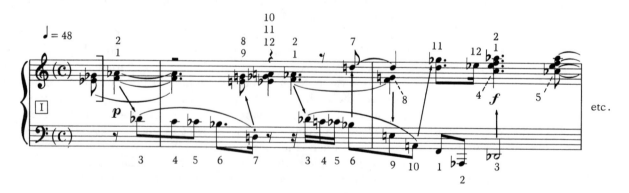

It will be seen that a number of tones in No. 3 are not numbered. They are therefore repetitions. Notice that the repetitions are of sections of melody as well as of single tones. The *a-flat, c, b,* and *b-flat* in measures 5 and 6 have been used earlier in the row. The row is not completed until the low tones in measure 6.

Opus 83, No. 3

The original and inverted forms are blended in the next excerpt. In order to present the structure as intelligibly as possible, the two series of numbers are separated by a staff. Dotted lines are inserted to clarify the sequences. Numbers in brackets indicate a tone occurring simultaneously in both rows. The inverted row drops the tenth tone (a♮) on the third time around (measure 13).

Opus 83, No. 5

No. 10, a combination of the original, retrograde, and inverted retrograde forms, requires no comment. It is noteworthy for the many repeated tones.

Opus 83, No. 10

The last of the pieces shows an interweaving of all four of the forms. Four parallel lines with the numbers are placed below the music. Numbers are related to tones directly above.

Opus 83, No. 12

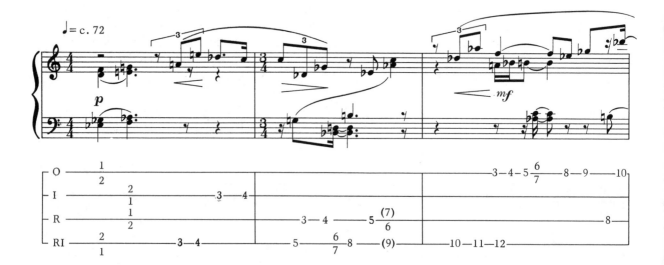

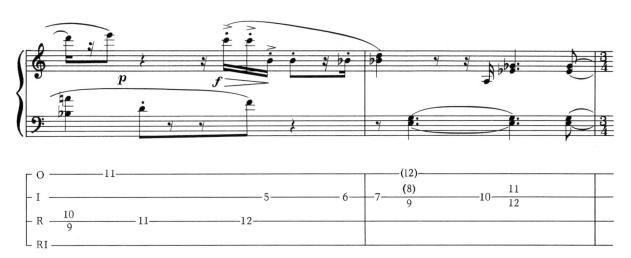

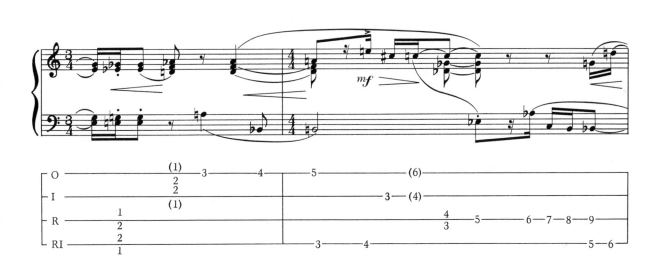

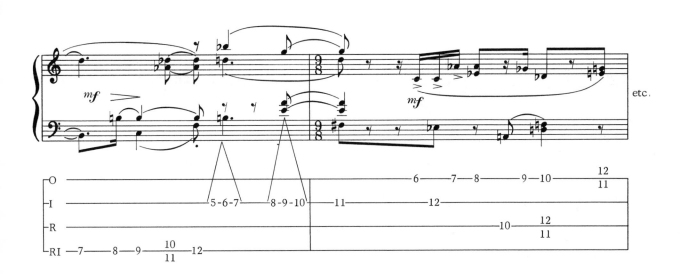

Once there is a thorough understanding of serial methods, analyses of the type just made are probably more time-consuming than rewarding. More important elements in formal analysis are, as they always have been, motives, phrases, phrase groups, and whole parts, and their disposition and interrelationships. With all the liberties and possibilities available to serialist composers there is no sure aural distinction between serial music and atonality in general. Schoenberg was the first to point out that the difference was much smaller than the public realized.

Those who wish to pursue the analysis of such music will enjoy Schoenberg's Concerto for Violin, his Fourth String Quartet, or the first and last movements of Alban Berg's *Lyric Suite*.

BARBER

Advances in Form

Example 155.   Barber, Concerto for Piano and Orchestra, Opus 38[3]

This concerto is a strong reminder that a thoroughly twentieth-century work is in no way hampered by a strict conformity to classical designs. No one of the three movements poses any formal problem. But composers endowed with originality have personal ways of using old forms, as we have seen in one example after another and will see again in the present instance. The style of writing links this music with the past more than is usually the case in contemporary composition. Possessed with an extraordinary gift for melody the composer was under no compulsion to depend on esoteric formulas or systems. At the same time, his inventiveness in presenting his material in ever-new guises enabled him to build a work in large form out of relatively few ideas. His manner of writing for the piano and the mastery of motivic development remind one of Liszt.

The first movement (Allegro appassionato), in sonata-form, begins with a short introduction for the soloist unaccompanied. It is expository in a very concentrated degree. The three most important motives (the first of phrase length) are heard within the first seven measures.

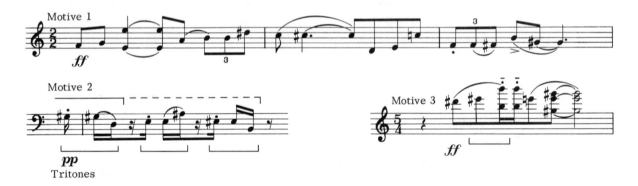

There are definite thematic kinships binding these motives, which become clear after a little examination. Compare the third motive with the opening notes of the first and the tritones of the second with that of the third. The nucleus of the second motive is three notes which in themselves constitute a motive, but since it is so often heard in combinations of three, a longer motive can be sensed (see dotted line). This interval of the tritone, spelled either as an augmented fourth or a diminished fifth, plays an important formative role throughout the movement. Observe these two flights for the piano, both of which grow out of Motive 2.[4]

---

[3] Copyright 1962 by G. Schirmer, Inc., New York. Used by permission.

[4] Intentional or not, the tritone figures in the sequence of keys of the three movements: E minor, C-sharp minor, B-flat minor.

Introduction

The primary theme, in elementary three-part form, is first heard in the orchestra.

Notice that the line of the accompaniment is derived from the theme. The cadence is a colorful modern adaptation of a medieval type, two diverging voices approaching a cadence point in stepwise movement, in this case, $f\natural-d\sharp$ to the octave on e. This theme is immediately transposed and restated but shared with the soloist who supplies a free canon in counterpoint to the orchestra during the second part.

The restatement of the primary theme passes, without cadencing, into an extension of thirteen measures during all of which the derivative accompanimental line, mentioned above, continues. This is followed by twenty measures devoted mainly to Motive I. Echos of Motive 3 are heard, as well as free figurations flavored with the tritone. All this is a departure from usual sonata practice, but it reflects the contemporary readiness to introduce developmental passages or sections at almost any point in the structure.

The subordinate theme arrives in G-sharp minor. Its contour invites comparison with Motive 1. The two ideas are sometimes placed end to end.

The "regular" development can be subdivided into eight sections according to the order in which materials are developed. The eighth section is a cadenza based almost wholly on the primary theme. The remainder of the movement adheres to the pattern set in the exposition.

The student should be able to supply answers to the following questions if a score is available:

1. Are there any noteworthy differences between the "expositional" development (measures 58–77) and its counterpart in the recapitulation?
2. Is there anything unusual about the position of the cadenza as compared to classical models?
3. What common melodic alteration occurs in Section V of the development?
4. Approximately how many measures make up the coda and how many sections are there?
5. Are all the principal motives used in the coda?
6. Study the following incidental figurations[5] and explain their derivation.

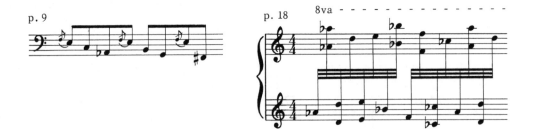

[5] Page numbers as in two-piano reduction, Schirmer.

p. 27

p. 36

p. 38

p. 39

The second movement (Canzone) is based on a single continuous melody. The form is essentially unipartite; however, the melody is repeated with some modification.

$$\overline{\underset{(1)\ (2-14)\ (15-20)\ (21-29)}{A}}\quad\overline{\underset{(30-42)\ (43-51)}{A^2}}$$

The six measures, 15–20 inclusive, bring no thematic contrast and are omitted in the repetition. Melodically, measures 2–14 and 30–42 are identical as are 21–29 and 43–51. Variety is obtained by much use of decorative passage work in the piano part and the alternation of phrases between the soloist and the orchestra. What must have suggested the accompanimental line in the first half of this movement?

The third movement (Allegro molto) is in simple rondo form. A quintuple meter (5/8) is maintained throughout.

CARTER

Example 156.   Carter, *Variations for Orchestra*[6]

This work, dating from 1955, has attracted much favorable attention and has added to the already enviable reputation of this American composer. Its points of originality are many. The theme is preceded by an introduction, though this in itself is no novelty. (See, for example, Beethoven's *Eroica Variations* or Rachmaninoff's Rhapsody for Piano and Orchestra.) However, Carter's introduction anticipates the theme in presenting several important ideas, including a phrase which generates the principal lyric element of the entire work. The section which is expressly designated as the theme is quite unlike the traditional period or double-period to which we are accustomed. Instead, we have 47 measures which might aptly be described as a series of musical suggestions that the composer will keep more or less in mind as he proceeds to the construction of a set of very free variations. At once we arrive at a counterpoint of pitches and contrasting note values which combine to produce the. characteristic textural language of this composer.

Carter assists the performers by indicating primary, secondary, and tertiary voices—that is, passages to be stressed in that order—by inserting the letters *A, B,* or *C* here and there in the score. Adopting this as a cue, we transcribe the first 17 measures of the theme (including the final two measures of the introduction), limiting the quotation to passages marked with an *A*. This will afford some idea of the diversity of the material. Although this music is atonal, serialism plays no part in it.

[6] Copyright 1957 by Associated Music Publishers, Inc., New York. Used by permission.

Metric Modulation

Analytical interest will immediately center on the imaginative treatment of rhythm and meter, especially on the device which the composer calls "metric modulation." As a technique this means the gradual moving from one set of metric values to another. Good examples may be seen in Variations 4 and 6. In the first of these variations, every four measures, running consecutively, form a group. The same "modulation," as counted in time, takes place in every group. In every "first" measure a quarter note is equal to 200 (MM) but becomes, in every "fourth" measure, equal to 119 (MM).

Measures 33–37 of Variation 4 (245–249 of the score) are quoted below. The first measure of the following group is included to show the smooth manner of joining the groups. These recurring junctures between slow ($\quarternote = 119$ MM) and fast ($\quarternote = 200$ MM) are perhaps the most fascinating feature of the variation.

The repeated cycles form a sort of metric ostinato. The oboe, moving from quarters to eighths to sixteenths, tends to offset the lengthening beat. The bassoon and viola, as well as the oboe, have sixteenths at the end of the fourth measure. It is intended that these notes at this point should exactly equal in duration the eighths to the right of the double bar. The mathematical ratio of the metronomic markings makes this quite clear. There should, therefore, be no perceptible break in movement in entering the next group. The composer provides very specific directions for the conductor on this point.

(Cl. omitted)

Variation 6 shows the reverse form of the device. The groups are now made up of six measures, an unessential detail. Two complete groups and one measure of the third are quoted not only to clarify the technique but to throw some light on the structural plan of the variation.

The clarinet passes into the triplet eighths of the next group as though the accelerando were continuing in quarters. Notice that the notation from that point is progressively augmented. Compare with the progressive diminution in Variation 4 and explain the reasons for the augmentation. At the beginning of the second group (i.e., measure 7 of the variation) the cello enters in imitation of the clarinet. Over the twelve measures the clarinet completes a long phrase which serves as a theme for the variation. At the tenth measure of the quotation the oboe enters playing dotted halves, which flow into the following quarters without change of duration. Examination of the full score will show that the cello in turn completes the phrase, while the oboe surrenders to the flute. The viola, bassoon, solo violin, and clarinet follow at various time intervals. The phrase may be started in one group and completed in the next, but due to the controlled tempo the effect in durations is approximately equalized. Tension and complexity mount as the variation draws to a close, and one sees in both variations a new kind of metric counterpoint. Incidentally, in both variations the scoring is for woodwinds and strings with a sparing use of the harp in Variation 6.

Elsewhere the composer is very frequently preoccupied with built-in accelerandos and ritardandos, accomplished by changing note values without specified alterations in basic tempo. The following flights are typical.

The effecting of a ritardando or an accelerando by graduated augmentation or diminution of note durations was well-known to the old masters. (See Beethoven's Sonata Opus 90, first movement, approaching the recapitulation, or the coda of Brahms's Rhapsody (for piano), Opus 79, No. 2.)[7] But it was used only in an incidental way. In Elliott Carter's *Variations* we see it elevated to a major element of musical structure. For other examples of "metric modulation" see Carter's String Quartet, No. 2. Reference will be made to similar constructions in our discussion of Messiaen's *Vingt Regards*.

In basic form these variations offer little that is new. One may observe that the process of variation itself is more continuous than we find in the old style sets, a fact to be expected in a contemporary work. Some variations are fused as in a passacaglia, while others are cadenced. Because of the sharp contrasts of materials within the theme, it is not difficult to determine the source of most later developments. It is nevertheless an intricate score, due primarily to the composer's obvious liking for polyrhythms.

MESSIAEN

Example 157. Messiaen, *Vingt Regards sur l'Enfant-Jesus*[8]

This gigantic work for piano was composed during the Second World War. Because of its length, requiring about two and a half hours, it is seldom heard in its entirety. The title *(Twenty Contemplations of the Infant Jesus)* reflects the deep, religious nature of the man who wrote it. As music religiously-inspired, it is not what one would expect. The effects are at times tender and contemplative, but again thunderous and even brutal. It is appropriate as a study in forms and formative techniques because of Messiaen's contributions, especially in the area of rhythm, and because his music has had a far-reaching influence on the present generation of composers.

New techniques are present here and there but they are outnumbered by old techniques developed beyond all previous experience. Both old and new are easily understood, and the characteristic adaptations and advances can be readily explained to all students. Because of the length of the work we must restrict our attention to those techniques or devices which are used with greatest frequency.

New Ways with Rhythm

The music of *Vingt Regards* roams freely between tonality and atonality, with the latter generally in command. Key signatures (most often F-sharp major) are affixed to several of the pieces, but ties to tonality are invariably weakened by the constant chromatics and dissonant sonorities. Barlines are placed solely as rhythm (not meter) dictates. There are no time signatures. This is, of course, a return to medieval practice.

[7] See also the opening of Sibelius' Fourth Symphony (Example 117).

[8] Permission for reprint granted by Durand et Cie., Paris, copyright owners, and Elkan-Vogel Co., Inc., Philadelphia, agents.

Number 3 in the series ("L'échange") illustrates Messiaen's unique use of *agrandissement asymetrique,* that is, progressive asymmetrical enlargement of figurations through interval manipulation. The piece is definitely in unipartite form and all motivic materials are introduced in the first two measures.

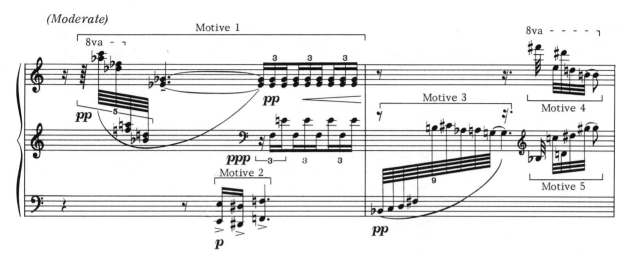

These measures, with all motives holding their position, are repeated eleven times without interruption. There are, however, certain pitch and interval alterations. Motive I never changes but Motives 2 and 3 are enlarged with each repetition, while Motive 4 becomes smaller. Motives 4 and 5 are the same, one being an inversion of the other, but are treated as separate motives here to avoid confusion. Successive soundings of Motive 3 are pitched a half-tone higher so that it eventually travels through the complete chromatic scale. Motive 5 moves parallel with Motive 3. Conversely, Motive 4 moves downward, also completing the chromatic cycle.[9] Thus we finally arrive at:

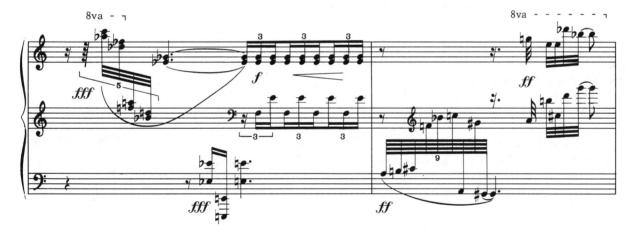

Messiaen's interest in tonal intensities accounts for the dynamic balance among the motives, which is preserved through a general crescendo that continues to the final cadence.

Number 5 ("Regard du Fils sur le Fils") has as the center of interest a "rhythm canon," which is heard as a ritornello in an overall rondo design. The first phrase is quoted along with its imitation. Notice that there is no identity of melody, but only of rhythm. There is another notable feature—the lower voice is in augmentation and at a most unusual ratio, all sounds are lengthened by one half their first value. Inevitably this leads to some abstruse notation. For greater clarity, only melody tones are shown. The lines connect corresponding sounds and rhythms.

---

[9] The piece is a bit of symbolism. Motive *A,* according to the composer, represents the unchanging deity while the other motives depict man in his ascent to godliness.

This is also an example of Messiaen's brand of polymodality. Attracted to oriental and other pentatonic modes, he used two such modes—

Number 6 ("Par Lui tout a été fait") is a fugue with a short subject and one countersubject. The question of whether it is a tonal or real fugue is not considered; it is in no way a conventional fugue. Only once in twenty-one pages of music does the subject reappear in its first form. It undergoes almost every imaginable mutation of pitch, intervals, rhythm, and register. Retrogression and melodic inversions are used liberally, alone or combined with other techniques.

The first nine measures afford a fair idea of Messiaen's manner of thematic metamorphosis through changes of rhythms and registers.

The subject as sounded in the answering voice follows the first version in scale order *only* (i.e., *d♯, e, f, f♯*, etc.); changes in rhythm, register, and time values utterly transform it. The small (grace) notes become primary notes. The subject immediately goes into an ostinato. Even here changes occur: the initial tone is pitched a half-step lower with each measure while others are progressively pitched higher. The *b* and *a♯* remain fixed. A single note replaces the repeated notes. In short, we have another example of Messiaen's asymmetrical enlargement.

Several canons are heard, of which the following is especially intriguing. In conventional terms it is a stretto on the subject although this may not be recognized at first. Messiaen describes this canon as *de rythmes non-rétrogradables*, meaning that its rhythm patterns are the same read forward or backward. There are three such patterns and no two are alike. In each we see a long "free" tone in the center. (It is safer to speak of tones here rather than notes.) The shorter tones to left and right of the central tone are similar in value but in reverse order, hence the term *non-rétrogradable* (non-reversible). Viewing the passage as a canon, the pitch interval between voices—a minor second—and the time interval—equivalent to an eighth note—are of more than incidental interest.

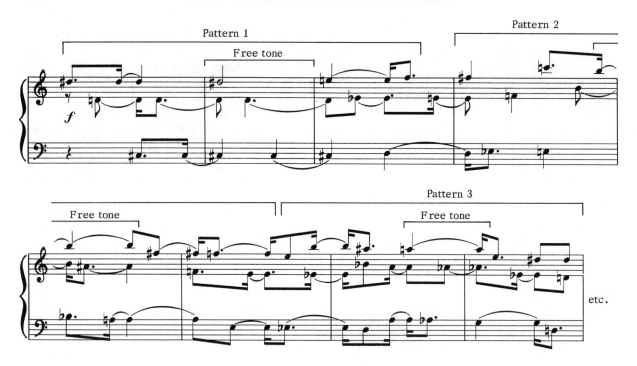

Other favorite devices of this composer are the alternate contrasting of groups of notes of very short value and groups of very long value, and the expansion of motives by adding notes both to the right and left. Quite naturally, Messiaen understands metric modulation and uses it often, although he does not label it as such. In Number 18 of this series of pieces may be found an unusual exhibition of accelerated versus retarded values *(valeurs progressivement accélérées et ralenties)*. It is represented below atonally.

Notes within any bracket represent a continuous sound, and dotted lines are barlines. The basic plan of these self-accelerating and retarding lines in such a combination is as simple as playing a theme against a retrograde version of itself. Messiaen's touch is seen in the *smallness* of the changes of value from one sound to the next, in every case the equivalent of a sixteenth note.

The influence of Messiaen among musicians of this generation is well known. The importance of such works as *Vingt Regards* could well be greater than the intrinsic worth of the music itself because of possibilities revealed to other composers. Composition has become international to a degree unmatched in all the history of music. Ideas, theories, and trends are shared around the world. Only a book devoted to contemporary music could do the subject justice, but enough has been presented to refute the claim that a "new" music, free of all ties with the past, is coming into being. There are always new ideas, new styles and, more rarely, a new technique. But, as may be seen in the case of Messiaen, even the most startling procedures usually have a history that reaches back into earlier centuries.

Of all elements of music, form has been affected least. From all the diversity of styles and methods a few general facts emerge. Textures have become more contrapuntal compared to the nineteenth century, which encourages such forms as the fugue, the passacaglia, and variations. Other influences have furthered the trend, such as atonality, chromaticism, and the abandonment of old styles of metric-harmonic accompaniment. There is less sealing of parts with prescribed cadences; indeed, the modern treatment of cadences allows a composer to be a composer until the final note and not a copyist. The old dance influence no longer stalks through compositions, measuring off a melody with a ballroom yard stick. There is a closer rapport between phrases, and phrasing is done with little regard for symmetry or mathematics. With the relaxing of meter has come a healthy return to an older and more fundamental conception of rhythm.

But not everything has changed. The motive has not only held its own but has been accentuated. Also, the laws of variety and repetition are still in force. Finally, there are laws of reason which, in the end, prevail. To every extremism there is always a reaction—movements in the history of composition bearing such names as neo-classicism or neo-romanticism sprang from a reactionary impulse. The creation of music is a continuous human endeavor in which thousands participate. It may be swayed by this force or that, but it will go forward.

Index of Musical Examples

Examples, from motive length to full movements, have been taken from music listed below. In some cases only graphs appear. Example numbers are in parentheses.

239

General Index